CAMBRIDGE INTRODUCTION TO WORLD HISTORY
GENERAL EDITOR · TREVOR CAIRNS

G000131046

The British Welfare State 1900–1950

Sydney Wood

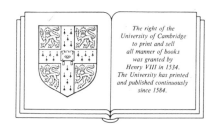

The right of the
University of Cambridge
to print and sell
all manner of books
was granted by
Henry VIII in 1534.
The University has printed
and published continuously
since 1584.

CAMBRIDGE UNIVERSITY PRESS
Cambridge
New York   New Rochelle
Melbourne   Sydney

Published by the Press Syndicate of the University of Cambridge
The Pitt Building, Trumpington Street, Cambridge CB2 1RP
32 East 57th Street, New York, NY 10022, USA
10 Stamford Road, Oakleigh, Melbourne 3166, Australia

© Cambridge University Press 1982

First published 1982
Third printing 1987

Printed in Great Britain at the
University Press, Cambridge

Library of Congress catalogue card number: 81–3840

British Library cataloguing in publication data
Wood, Sydney
The British welfare state, 1900–1950.–
(Cambridge introduction to the history of
mankind)
1. Great Britain – Social policy
I. Title
361.6′5′0941   HN385
ISBN 0 521 22843 3

Portrait drawings by Ian Newsham
Diagrams by Andrew Harden

Illustrations in this volume are reproduced by kind permission of the following: Front cover, pp. 7, 22, 26 London Borough of Tower Hamlets, Local History Collection; Back cover, pp, 14, 21, 41 *Punch*; p. 4 Professor Andrew B. Semple; pp. 12, 35 The Greater London Council Photograph Library; pp. 16, 32, 37, 45 (below left and right) BBC Hulton Picture Library; p. 20 Cambridgeshire Collection; p. 40 (left) The Labour Party; p. 40 (right) The Conservative Research Department; p. 45 (above) Mirror Group Newspapers; p. 46 Harlow Council.

Front cover: *Women and children carry away bread that has been supplied to them by the Poor Law guardians in Poplar, one of London's poorest districts. The photograph was taken in 1920. The Poplar authorities were known to be more generous than most others.*

Back cover: *A 'Punch' cartoon of December 1942 shows the high hopes raised by Sir William Beveridge's report on 'Social Insurance and Allied Services', published on 2 December. Beveridge estimated that to provide everyone with protection against unemployment, illness and old age would cost £697 million, to be shared by workers, employers and the state.*

Note on money before 1971
£1 = 20s (shillings)
1s = 12d (pence)

Contents

Introduction

Today we tend to take it for granted that people too old or ill to work should not be left to starve, that schooling should be provided for all children and that there should be doctors and hospitals to care for the sick. Any British government today is expected to do its best to see that as few as possible of those able to work are without jobs and to make sure that there are homes for all. Welfare services like these cost a huge amount of money and need a vast army of officials to make them work. Only the state can provide for all these needs and this book is an account of how and why Britain built up its welfare state in the twentieth century.

1 In darkest Britain, 1905

Early-twentieth-century Britain was one of the world's mightiest powers. Vast stretches of several continents had been conquered to form the British Empire. Britain's navy was the most formidable afloat and her industries churned out goods that supplied markets around the globe.

Yet many of the country's leaders were worried about conditions within Britain. Some of these worries were voiced by the Liberal politician H. H. Asquith when he said, 'What is the use of talking about Empire if here, at its very centre, there is always to be found a mass of people stunted in education, congested beyond the possibility of realising in any true sense either social or domestic life?'

One of Asquith's colleagues, Winston Churchill, expressed very similar feelings, declaring: 'I see little glory in an Empire which can rule the waves and is unable to flush its own sewers!'

Widespread poverty

There was, by the twentieth century, no excuse for Britain's leaders not to know a good deal about the problems to which Asquith and Churchill were referring. During the late nineteenth century parliament had set up a whole series of investigations into aspects of working-class life and work. To the evidence gathered by officials could be added the articles and books produced by journalists, church ministers, and wealthy individuals whose consciences were deeply troubled by the poverty that they saw in their own country.

Housing was one area where both private and official investigations had turned up a most gloomy mass of evidence. In 1885 a Royal Commission had concluded: 'It is quite certain that the working classes are largely housed in dwellings

Many of Britain's cities contained slum houses in 1900 like these homes in Liverpool. The families each have one or two rooms that lead onto an open courtyard: two lavatories at the back of the yard serve all the families.

The average expectation of life in England and Wales

	Men	Women
1881	44 years	47 years
1900	46 years	50 years
1910	52 years	55 years
1951	66 years	72 years

that would be unsuitable even if they were not overcrowded. The old houses are rotten from age and neglect. The new ones are rotten from the first.' Efforts to build better houses in the next twenty years had barely begun to solve the housing problem.

In 1889 G. R. Sims tried to stir the consciences of the wealthy by reporting on his exploration of a part of London inhabited by the poor which he saw as 'a dark continent that is within easy walking distance of the General Post Office'. Sims believed that there was no need for the rich to go great distances to explore the unknown areas of the 'dark continent' of Africa: an equally unknown one lay on their own doorsteps. His report was full of accounts of visits to homes like this. 'What a room! The walls are damp and crumbling, the ceiling is black and peeling off, the floor is rotten and broken away in places and the wind and rain sweep in through gaps. The woman, her husband, and her six children live and sleep in this one room.'

Thousands of people in Britain, such writers suggested, simply could not afford a few rooms for themselves and their families. In the cramped quarters they could afford, lavatories and clean water supplies were commonly not provided for each home. Instead, many families shared quite inadequate facilities.

Booth and Rowntree

That so much was known about poverty in early-twentieth-century Britain was due particularly to the work of two men. Liverpool shipowner Charles Booth spent the years 1889 to 1903 studying the poor of London and publishing his findings in the seventeen volumes of *Life and Labour of the People in London*. In 1899 Seebohm Rowntree, son of the famous chocolate manufacturer, carried out a similar study in his home town of York and published it as *Poverty: A Study of Town Life*. Both men worked out how much a family of five would need to earn to stay just beyond a life of starvation. Rowntree reckoned that twenty-one shillings and eight pence (21s 8d) a week would be just enough as long as the money was spent very carefully. The family (he wrote)

'Must never spend a penny on railway fare or omnibus. They must never purchase a half penny newspaper or

A week's budget for a Middlesborough family of three, 1907
(Evidence collected by Lady Bell)

	s	d
Rent	5	6
Coals	2	4
Insurance		7
Meat	1	6
Clothing	1	—
1 stone flour	1	5
¼ stone bread meal		2½
1 lb butter	1	1
½ lb lard		2½
1 lb bacon		9
4 lbs sugar		8
½ lb tea		9
Yeast		1
Milk		3
1 box polish		1
1 lb soap		3
1 pkt washing powder		1
3 oz tobacco		9
½ stone potatoes		3
Onions		1
Matches		1
Lamp oil		2
Debt		3
	18	6

Seebohm Rowntree. 1871–1954. Member of wealthy York chocolate manufacturing family. Chairman of the firm 1925–41. Determined to apply his Christian beliefs to both public and business life. Very concerned about the problem of poverty and reforms best-suited to tackling poverty. Published three widely read studies of poverty in York in 1901, 1941 and 1951. Interested in other social problems, including the reform of agriculture, the needs of old people, and the problem of gambling.

spend a penny to buy a ticket for a popular concert. They must write no letters. They must never contribute to church or chapel or give help to a neighbour. They cannot save nor can they join sick club or trade union. The children must have no pocket money. The father must smoke no tobacco and must drink no beer. The mother must never buy any pretty clothes. Should a child fall ill it must be attended by the parish doctor; should it die it must be buried by the parish. The wage earner must never be absent from his work for a single day.'

Booth and Rowntree found not only that the elderly and those without work lived miserably poor lives, but that many workers were paid wages so low that they could not afford life's bare necessities. They noted countless cases like this railwayman whom Rowntree met and who was wearing 'a patched coat that cannot possibly hold together much longer. He has walked 28 miles today in search of work with only a crust of bread for breakfast and more bread for supper. His feet, half hidden by the apologies for shoes, are blistered and swollen, his attitude is of a man who is giving up all hope.'

Having finished his own study and read Booth's work, Rowntree reached a conclusion that horrified him: 'We are faced with the startling probability', he wrote, 'that from twenty-five to thirty per cent of the town populations of the United Kingdom are living in poverty.'

Friendly Societies

During the later nineteenth century many of those skilled workers able to put aside savings from their wages paid weekly sums to organisations called Friendly Societies. In this way the Societies were able to gather funds upon which people could draw when too old or ill to work. Some trade unions also gathered savings for such purposes, especially unions like the Amalgamated Society of Engineers that were formed to serve skilled workers. By the 1900s the savings put into unions and Friendly Societies had grown to the impressive figure of £40 million. But most workers could not afford such savings. It did not take much to bring disaster to ordinary families, an illness or a business slump throwing men out of work could do it.

The workhouses

People made hopelessly poor by circumstances beyond their control had long been a cause of concern to those running both central government and local affairs. Local areas were required by the government to raise money (called a poor rate) by taxing the better off and to use it to provide for the aged, the orphaned, the sick and sometimes those out of work. Poor Law Unions were set up all over the country and built workhouses to house the poor. Conditions in workhouses were deliberately made so harsh that no one who could find a job would think it worthwhile not working.

In 1892 the Labour politician George Lansbury visited the Poplar Workhouse and wrote, afterwards,

'It was easy for me to understand why the poor dreaded and hated these places, all these prison sort of surroundings were organized for the purpose of making decent people endure any suffering rather than enter. Sick and aged, lunatics and babies and children, able bodied and tramps, all herded together in one huge range of buildings. Clothing was of the usual workhouse type, plenty of corduroy and blue cloth. No undergarments for either men or women, boots worn till they fell off. On one visit I inspected the supper of oatmeal porridge served up

Old ladies in Poplar workhouse in 1908.

Numbers in workhouses in England and Wales

1871	143,000
1886	186,000
1896	214,000

with pieces of black stuff floating around. We discovered it to be rat and mice manure.'

Workhouses varied, some tried to treat the poor with decency and to provide a reasonable diet.

In 1905 Mrs Beatrice Webb, a lady from a rich family who had decided to devote herself to trying to reform life for ordinary folk in Britain, described some of the sights she and her fellow members of a Royal Commission had observed:

'We have seen feeble minded boys growing up in the workhouse, year after year, untaught and untrained, alternately neglected and tormented by the other inmates. We have seen idiots who are physically offensive or so noisy as to create a disturbance by day and by night, living in the ordinary wards. We have seen half-witted women nursing the sick, feeble minded women put in charge of babies, and imbecile old men put to look after the boys out of school hours. We have seen expectant mothers who have come in for their confinements working, eating and sleeping in close companionship with idiots and imbeciles of revolting habits and hideous appearance.'

Beatrice Webb (née Potter). 1858–1943. The daughter of a wealthy family, she became increasingly concerned with social problems, helped Charles Booth study London's poor, and published a study of the Co-operative Movement. In 1892 she married Sidney Webb (Baron Passfield in 1929) and together they worked hard for social reforms and for the Labour Party. Served on Royal Commissions on the Poor Law, Trade Unions and Coal Mines. Helped start *The New Statesman* 1913 and the London School of Economics (1895). The Webbs published books on trade unionism and on local government.

Yet the workhouses of 1905 were less severe than they had once been. Rules had been relaxed a little to prevent the forcible separation of elderly couples and to allow the aged the comforts of a little tea and tobacco. The beginnings of a hospital system to care for ordinary people could be seen in the infirmaries set up by some of the workhouses in larger cities: to them went local people not in fact in workhouses. Even so workhouses remained places feared by the poor. A Manchester alderman argued, in 1905, that the poor 'have the daily fear that the workhouse must be the final refuge and this fear is harder to bear than the pinch of hunger, the cold of insufficient clothing or the poverty of their surroundings'.

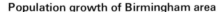

The population of Britain (excluding Ireland)

1841	18,500,000
1861	23,100,000
1881	29,700,000
1901	37,000,000
1951	48,900,000

Government action

The huge population growth of nineteenth-century Britain had led to a crowding together of people in unhealthy conditions in towns and cities. Terrible outbreaks of disease persuaded the government to urge local authorities to clean up their water supplies in order to prevent cholera, and to introduce compulsory vaccination to get rid of smallpox. Working conditions in mines and factories were regulated to remove the very worst abuses of overlong hours spent in needlessly dangerous surroundings. From 1870 the government mounted a campaign to persuade children to go to school and set up local School Boards that would provide education for all the children in their areas. So, as the *Economist* magazine noticed in 1895, 'Little by little and year by year the fabric of state expenditure is built up like a coral island.'

How to solve this huge problem of poverty troubled the minds of the investigators who studied the poor; in 1883 the Congregational minister Andrew Mearns reached a conclusion shared by several other investigators when he argued, 'The State must secure for the poorest the rights of citizenship, the right to live as something better than the uncleanest of brute beasts.'

The rulers of Britain were far from convinced that it was their job to remove poverty. They were not used to passing laws to organise people's lives in detail; they suspected that the cost would mean taxes too high to be accepted by taxpayers; and they did not have large numbers of officials at their command to carry out a huge programme of reforms.

More pressures for change

The belief that Britain contained too much poverty, disease, and ignorance was not just a matter of concern to people with

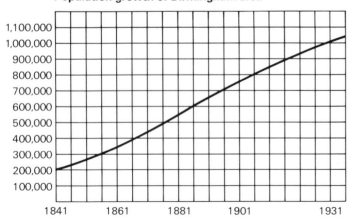

Population growth of Birmingham area

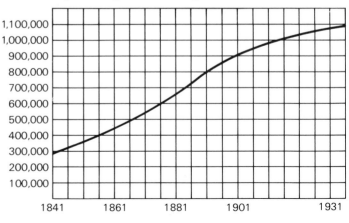

Population growth of Glasgow area

consciences about the plight of thousands of their fellow citizens; there were military, economic and political arguments for tackling the problem of poverty.

In 1902 the Boer War ended in British victory, but only after it had taken alarmingly long to crush the forces of a small South African state. The army was concerned about the health of recruits; one of the war's heroes, Robert Baden Powell, warned his newly formed Scout Movement in 1908, 'Recent reports on the deterioration of our race ought to act as a warning to be taken in time before it goes too far. One cause which contributed to the downfall of the Roman Empire was the fact that the soldiers fell away from the standard of their forefathers in bodily strength.'

The army had to turn down many city-dwellers who came to volunteer to fight in the Boer War even though it applied the lowest standards of health that it dared. In Manchester, for example, 12,000 volunteered, 8,000 were rejected at once and of the remainder only 1,200 were eventually accepted. Such a sign of military weakness was especially worrying at a time when European states were building up their armed forces and quarrelling increasingly often.

There also seemed reason to believe that the poor health and education of workers played a part in the decline of Britain as an industrial country when compared to other lands. By 1900 both the USA and Germany produced more than the British steel industry. Britain lagged well behind these two lands in developing new industries based on electricity, chemicals and the internal combustion engine; these were complex industries requiring a better educated workforce than was needed to cut coal or supervise a loom. It was American skill and materials that built London's first electric tube train in 1890: even the new uniforms worn by the British army in the later stages of the Boer War were coloured khaki by a dye obtained from Germany.

The two main political parties in Britain were the Liberals and the Conservatives, but they were under pressure from other groups seeking to tackle Britain's social problems. Trade unions, set up to improve conditions for their members, were growing and vigorously organising strikes and demonstrations against poor working conditions. In 1892 trade union membership was 1,576,000, by 1900, 2,022,000. A number of Socialist societies had appeared. In 1899 several Socialist leaders met some trade union leaders to set up a Labour Representation committee. Their aim was to work for a distinct group of Labour members of parliament to represent their interests: in 1900 they managed to get two of their number elected. All this activity persuaded some Liberals and Conservatives that they had to do something to prevent workers searching for solutions that might injure the political system and even seriously upset peace in Britain.

In 1905 a group of experts delivered a report to MPs that expressed the feeling that poverty was damaging: 'No country, however rich, can permanently hold its own in the race of international competition if hampered by an increasing load of this dead weight [of poverty] or can successfully perform the role of sovereignty beyond the seas if a portion of its own folk at home are sinking below the civilisation of its subject races abroad.'

Summary of Key Steps

1889–1903 Charles Booth wrote *Life and Labour of the People in London*
1899–1901 Seebohm Rowntree wrote *Poverty: a study of Town Life*
1899–1902 Boer War

2 Lloyd George's ambulance wagon

The Royal Commission on the Poor Laws, 1905–9

On 4 December 1905, the Conservative government resigned after ten years in office. One of its last acts, on its very last day, was to gather a group of experts to form a Royal Commission to study the Poor Laws and recommend changes. Though the Conservatives then lost the general election of 1906 to the Liberal Party, the Royal Commission went on collecting evidence and discussing possible changes until it finally produced a report in 1909.

The Commission included Poor Law guardians, officials from a government department called the Local Government Board, Labour leaders and Poor Law experts (one of whom was Charles Booth). The commissioners divided on what they thought should be done. Ten of them wanted to see the existing system overhauled to give more power to local authorities and to increase efficiency. With all social services under the control of local Public Assistance Committees they thought a better system would emerge that would still make it very clear to the poor that, if at all possible, they were to fend for themselves. The Majority Report suggested that poverty might still be due to the personal faults of the poor.

But four commissioners disagreed. They were led by Beatrice Webb and signed a Minority Report drawn up by Beatrice's husband. Sidney Webb was not a Commission member, but he and his wife worked together for reforms that would greatly increase the power of the government. Their

Growth of local government

1871	Local Government Board set up to supervise public health and the many locally elected Poor Law guardians who, from 1834, supervised care of the poor; in Scotland the work was done by Parochial Boards, from 1845
1888	Elected county councils created
1893	Elected district and parish councils set up

report declared that poverty was caused not by the personal failings of poor people, but by the state of the economy of the country and the way the country was organised. They suggested that there should be a standard of living decided upon below which no one should slip. The task of coping with poverty should fall first on the government and everything possible should be done to help the poor find work and receive training for much-needed jobs. They asked for 'a national minimum of civilised life open to all alike of both sexes and all classes, sufficient nourishment and training when young, a living wage when able-bodied, treatment when sick and a modest but secure livelihood when disabled or aged'.

These reports, together with a mass of evidence about widespread poverty and the unsatisfactory way it was being tackled were presented to Liberal government ministers in 1909. By then these ministers were ready to listen to reformers who urged the need to tackle the problem of poverty.

The Liberal government

The election of 1906 had swept the Liberals to power with a massive majority. The results were Liberals 401 MPs, Conservatives 157, Labour 29, Irish Nationalists 83 (these last two groups usually supported the Liberals).

Among the new ministers, David Lloyd George proved especially ready to listen to pleas for reform. Lloyd George had been brought up in North Wales by his shoe-maker uncle, a background far more humble than that of his Cabinet colleagues. His upbringing alone did not determine his resolution to tackle social reform, he also believed (as he argued in 1906): 'If it were found that a Liberal Party had done nothing to cope seriously with the social condition of the people, to remove the slums and widespread poverty in a land glittering with wealth, then would a real cry arise in this land for a new party.'

David Lloyd George.
1863–1945. Born in Manchester, the son of Welsh parents, and brought up in North Wales from the age of two by his uncle, Richard Lloyd. Became a solicitor. 1890 elected Liberal M.P. for Caernarvon. A brilliant orator, a clever schemer, regarded as a very radical Liberal. Opposed Britain's war with the Boers. 1905–8 President of Board of Trade and 1908–15 Chancellor of the Exchequer. Played a leading part in bringing in National Insurance and old age pensions as well as battling against the House of Lords to secure higher taxes and a weaker upper chamber. Became a keen supporter of war effort 1914–18 and Prime Minister 1916–22. So involved with Irish and foreign affairs that his reputation as a social reformer slipped. From 1922 in Opposition, deeply distrusted by many politicians who thought him unprincipled and too fond of power. Supported research into radical policies for tackling unemployment.

Lloyd George was President of the Board of Trade till 1908, then Chancellor of the Exchequer. His successor at the Board of Trade, Winston Churchill, came from a wealthy and privileged background, yet he too developed a great enthusiasm for social reform. A fellow Liberal, Charles Masterman, observed in 1908: 'He is full of the poor whom he has just discovered. He thinks he is called by Providence to do something for them.'

But the Prime Ministers – Campbell-Bannerman till 1908 and H. H. Asquith after that – had plenty of other problems to worry them. The idea of a really far-reaching reform to alter the whole way that poverty was dealt with in Britain was not something that most Liberals cared for: the Royal Commission reports were read, put aside, and allowed to gather dust. Within the government the President of the Local Government Board, John Burns, defended the existing system declaring: 'The Poor Law is in a new atmosphere; it is sympathetic, progressive, reasonable, and adaptable to any sensible demand that may be made on it.' So, for one reason or another, the Liberal government preferred to change the existing system gradually. But Lloyd George did not give up. As he told a large audience in Birmingham in 1911: 'I have joined the Red Cross. I am in the Ambulance Corps. I am engaged to drive a waggon through the twistings and turnings and ruts of the Parliamentary road. I am in a hurry for I can hear the moanings of the wounded and I want to carry relief to them in the alleys, the homes, where they lie stricken.'

Opponents of change

Lloyd George's ambulance had to get past people eager to block its path. As we have seen relieving poverty was likely to mean higher rates and taxes and more officials; this alone was enough to anger those Conservatives who felt it was the government's responsibility to interfere in people's lives as little as possible. This point of view received support from those who were already running organisations to help people guard themselves against times of hardship. The insurance companies and Friendly Societies feared that if the state became more active in tackling poverty, it would take over their work. An official of one of the biggest Friendly Societies, the Foresters, argued, 'The aim of the working class ought to be to bring about economic conditions in which there should be no need for distribution of state alms. Man is a responsible being. The working class should rise to the occasion and insist upon being capable of using their own wages to their own advantage.'

A writer in *The Times* newspaper referring to a suggestion that school meals be provided, believed that too much was being done already: 'We have already made a serious inroad upon personal responsibility and independence by relieving parents of the duty of educating their children', he wrote, 'That is now used as an argument for relieving them of the duty of feeding their children. When we have done that, the argument will be stronger than ever for relieving them of the duty of clothing their children.'

There were other people who did not like the way that Liberals planned to pay for part of some of their social reforms by taking money from workers' pay packets. The Labour Party included people who believed that the whole cost should be carried by the Treasury.

The most difficult part of the struggle to push through limited social reform was not in arguments in the country at large, but within parliament itself. Although the Liberals had a huge House of Commons majority, in the House of Lords the Conservatives were in control. The power of the Lords was considerable; they could alter or even totally reject bills passed by the Commons, and in the years after 1906 they used this power so often that many Liberals became frustrated and angry. When the Lords criticised the cost of Liberal reforms, Lloyd George compared some of its members to Britain's new battleships: 'A fully-equipped duke costs as much to keep as two dreadnoughts, and they are just as great a terror, and they last longer.'

Meals and medical inspections for children

Liberal reforms began with an attack on health problems that had worried many people for some years. The Boer War's exposure of the poor state of health of so many people had greatly strengthened a campaign that included among its demands the provision of school meals for needy children. The Conservatives had refused to listen to this campaign since the cost of reforms would mean increased rates or taxes. But the Liberal government readily responded to the campaign and in 1906 supported a Labour MP who proposed a bill allowing local education authorities to provide school meals. Parents able to pay for such meals were expected to do so but the act allowed meals to be provided free by schools: 'Where children are unable by reason of lack of food to take full advantage of education, they may apply to the Board of Education and spend out of the rates.' By 1913, however, over half the education authorities in England and Wales had still not begun to provide school meals.

The medical inspection of schoolchildren also attracted the campaigners for a healthy Britain. In 1907 a bill was successfully pushed through parliament requiring a regular checking of schoolchildren by doctors. The reports these doctors sent in led to such concern that school clinics were gradually introduced with (from 1912) help from government funds.

Parents had to struggle to get treatment for their children.

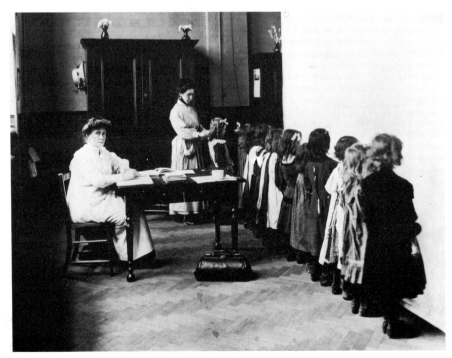

Medical inspection for schoolchildren, like this one taking place in 1911 in Deptford, showed up all sorts of diseases and deformities. Children's hair was often full of vermin. The nurse on the right is checking a class of girls for this problem.

In 1913 Dr Marion Philips described a common situation: 'A mother took her daughter to hospital for astigmatism. She had to wait there two hours. She has been twice so far and has to go again. The cost of these two visits, in addition to a "voluntary" contribution in the hospital box, is: glasses 5s 6d, fares 6s 8d, substitute for work 2s 6d, food while away 9d.'

At a time when families were hard put to it to manage on just over a pound a week, costs like these were a huge burden. Nor could school doctors do anything about conditions of poor housing, clothing and diet, that led to so much ill health. A few workhouses had infirmaries for the poor of the area; otherwise they had to depend on hospitals and clinics set up by charity. In the early twentieth century voluntary societies set up maternity and child welfare clinics. Not till 1914 did they get any finance from the government, nor were there enough of them.

The Children's Charter, 1908

In 1908 a young Liberal MP, Herbert Samuel, successfully steered through parliament a bill that gathered together a number of measures dealing with child welfare. The act was soon being popularly referred to as 'The Children's Charter'. Children were now forbidden to beg: when accused of offences they were to be tried in special Juvenile Courts and could be sent not to ordinary prisons but to special homes called 'borstals', away from adult criminals. A probation service was introduced. Children under sixteen were to be excluded from public houses and, the act laid down, 'if any person sells to a person under sixteen any cigarettes, he shall be liable to a fine not exceeding £2. It shall be the duty of a constable, or of a park keeper being in uniform, to seize any cigarettes in the possession of any person under the age of sixteen whom he finds smoking in the streets or public places.'

One working man grumbled that the forbidding of alcohol to the young was a mistake because, he thought,

'Tis just the way to drive 'em into drink, to make a forbidden mystery o' it. Chil'erns Charter do 'em call it? Mischief makers opportunity, I say! Some o' its all right, but half the time them that makes these laws don't know nort t'all 'bout it; we has to have 'em about 'long wi us kicking up their buzz, all the time. I reckon that them as can afford nurses to look after 'em an take 'em off their hands ought to have double punishment.'

Wealthy Conservatives were not the only people suspicious of the way rules and regulations and the power of officials were growing as a result of Liberal reforms.

Old age pensions, 1908

The idea of paying pensions to the elderly had been attracting support for many years before the Liberal government of 1906 was formed. Visitors to workhouses were especially saddened by the sight of old folk reduced, after a lifetime of labour, to living there simply because they were now too old to earn a living. Charles Booth organised and led a campaign in favour of a system of old age pensions paid for out of taxation and won trade union and Labour Party support. But the Liberals hesitated. The problem was not the principle of pensions, but the cost. A series of by-elections in which Labour candidates defeated Liberals finally encouraged the Liberals to act. The bill was presented to the Commons by Asquith, and piloted through by Lloyd George. The pensions were not generous, and were paid to people at the age of seventy, not at sixty-five (as many campaigners for pensions thought proper). The Liberals hastened to point out that though taxes would be needed to pay the pensions, the act would reduce the burden on rates by making it less likely that elderly people would turn to the Poor Law.

Flora Thompson remembered how the elderly had welcomed the pensions in her village,

'When old age pensions began, life was transformed for aged cottagers. They were relieved of anxiety; independence for life. At first when they went to the Post Office to draw it tears of gratitude would run down the cheeks of some and they would say as they picked up their money, "God bless that *Lord* George, and God bless you miss", and there were flowers from their gardens and apples from their trees for the girls who merely handed them the money.'

Though the pensions were small, they marked a big step forward. Going into the workhouse had meant not merely sorrow but, as a Poor Law official described it, 'loss of personal reputation, loss of personal freedom, and loss of political freedom by suffering disenfranchisement'. Elderly people who had lived in Britain for at least twenty years and had been

THE NEW YEAR'S GIFT.

The paying of pensions to people over seventy freed many of them from having to plead for help. This 'Punch' cartoon of January 1909 shows the year as a child bringing relief to a couple living in a very simple cottage.

KEY STEP: Old age pensions after 1908

Paid to people over 70 years old		Pension per week
Where yearly means do not exceed £21		5s
Where yearly means exceed £21,		
but do not exceed	£23 12s 6d	4s
	£26 5s 0d	3s
	£28 17s 6d	2s
	£31 10s 0d	1s
Pension for a married couple		10s

out of prison for the last ten of those years (a time-span later shortened to two) earned the right to a pension. Getting help was now, for the elderly, a right, not a badge of shame to be avoided if at all possible. Lloyd George had noticed, by 1911, 'The administration of the Old Age Pensions Act has revealed there is a mass of poverty which is too proud to wear the badge of pauperism.'

People too proud to go for poor relief were perfectly prepared to collect pensions at post offices: the state had significantly dented the scope of the Poor Law. Helping elderly folk beyond heavy labour was clearly different from helping the younger able-bodied people able to work, yet unable to find steady employment. Yet this too was an aspect of poverty the Liberals were prepared to tackle.

The battle over the budget

By 1909 the Liberals' reforms had added quite considerably to the country's tax burden. The old age pensions alone needed £8 million in a year and this at a time when the government had also decided to carry out a costly expansion of Britain's navy. As Chancellor of the Exchequer after 1908 the task of finding further revenue fell upon Lloyd George.

The Chancellor vigorously defended this big increase in taxes saying, 'This is a War Budget. It is for raising money to wage implacable warfare against poverty and squalidness. I cannot help hoping and believing that before this generation has passed away we shall have advanced a great step towards that good time when poverty and wretchedness shall be as remote to the people of this country as the wolves that once infested its forests.'

Feeling in the Conservative Party ran strongly against the budget. In the House of Lords, especially, landowners objected to the proposed land taxes and to the survey of their lands. To some Conservatives it was a Socialist budget, wrong in principle, others were soon stirred to attack the budget by the violent language used against landowners by the Chancellor of the Exchequer. 'Who made ten thousand people owners of the soil and the rest of us trespassers in the land of our birth?' he asked of an audience in Newcastle.

The Conservatives not only delayed the budget in the Commons for as long as possible, in November 1909 they used their control of the Lords to reject it completely by 350 votes

Target	to raise £16 million.
Proposals	Income tax to range from 9d to 1s 2d, an increase in tax for the better off, who had been paying 1s.
	Super tax of 6d in the pound on incomes over £3,000.
	Higher duties on tobacco, beer, spirits, petrol.
	A land tax of 20% paid when land changed hands on the unearned increase in land value.
	A duty of $\frac{1}{2}$d in the pound on the value of undeveloped land and minerals. (A complete valuation of land in Britain would be needed.)
	Child allowances of £10 a child for those earning less than £500 a year.

to 75. Without the money it needed to carry on, no government could stay in office. Asquith promptly called a general election. He told a gathering in London, in December 1909, 'I tell you quite plainly neither I nor any Liberal Minister supported by a majority in the House of Commons is going to submit again to the humiliations of the last four years.'

The Liberals won the election, though they had fewer MPs than before. They had, with Labour and Irish support still got clear control of the Commons. The budget was allowed through, but the Liberals were bent on making sure such an event never happened again. The government proposed to prevent the Lords altering or rejecting money bills: their power over other bills was to be reduced to the right to bring about a two year delay, not outright rejection. The furious resistance of the Lords to this only crumbled before a second election result, fought on this issue, and before a threat to use the King's rather unwilling promise to create so many new Liberal peers that the Conservative majority there would be quite destroyed. Thus the battle for social reform had become mixed up in a battle over the constitution itself. The Liberal victory meant that its future social reforms would probably pass more easily into law than had its earlier efforts.

The two elections of 1910

January 1910	275 Liberals	273 Conservatives
	40 Labour	
	82 Irish Nationalists	
December 1910	272 Liberals	272 Conservatives
	42 Labour	
	84 Irish	

Unemployment, 1910–11

In their search for solutions to social problems, some Liberals were prepared to look into the way other countries tackled similar difficulties. In Germany, in particular, they found policies worth considering. Like Britain, Germany had many towns and cities housing people who worked in industries. Lloyd George went there in 1908 to look at the way Germany had developed provisions for the needy much in advance of those in Britain.

Even before Lloyd George visited Germany, another social reformer, William Beveridge, had made the journey. Beveridge was deeply concerned about unemployment and from 1908 was well placed in a post in the Board of Trade, to urge ministers to act. He found that Winston Churchill, the Board's President, was easily persuaded to take up the cause (in Churchill's words) of 'the casual labourer who is lucky to get three or four days work in the week, who may often be out of a job for three or four weeks at a time, who in bad times goes under altogether and who in good times has no hope of security; this poor man is here as the result of economic causes which have been too long unregulated'. Trade unions that gathered in savings from members to pay out again during times of unemployment offered help to around one and a half million men; the rest of the country's workforce simply could not save for hard times.

This problem had already worried Conservative ministers when they were in power. Even though they disliked increased rates and taxes, they did pass an act in 1905 that allowed local authorities to raise rates of up to a penny in the pound to be used to provide work for unemployed people during times of distress in winter. These funds were to be used to supplement the Queen Alexandra charity appeal that had raised £153,000

Social welfare in Germany

1883	3 million workers and their families were paid weekly sums of money from funds built up from weekly contributions paid by employers and workers.
1884	Workers injured by accidents in mines and factories were provided with pensions paid for by employers.
1886	These two schemes were extended to cover seven million workers and their families.
1889	Old age pensions, at the age of 70, were provided from funds built up by workers, employers, and the state.

but Lloyd George thought little of this solution: 'Like a motor car without petrol, or only such petrol as it could beg on the road,' he called it. From Germany's experience Beveridge, Lloyd George, and (through them) Churchill were persuaded that the problem of short-term unemployment could best be tackled by two measures, the setting up of labour exchanges and the adoption of the insurance principle. Through a network of labour exchanges information could be spread about the needs of employers for particular workers, and the skills that particular workers could offer. 'A labour exchange', Beveridge argued, 'may do what in a single firm is done as between different departments. It may become the headquarters of a compact, mobile reserve of labour covering the enormous stagnant reserve which drifts about the streets today.'

In 1910 eighty-three labour exchanges opened their doors to the public under the general direction of Beveridge. Their numbers increased rapidly, but workers did not have to register there when unemployed, nor did employers have to notify the exchanges about vacancies for workers. The exchanges were made attractive to the out of work by providing in them facilities for washing and clothes-mending as well as refreshments. Their services seem to have been of considerable value to skilled workers; for the unskilled they had far less to offer.

For unemployed people the government also planned a system of weekly payments. The idea of an insurance scheme to which workers would contribute money and upon which they would draw in time of need was felt by both Lloyd George and Churchill to be the right one. Such a plan meant that people who did not qualify because they were not part of an insurance scheme, or who had used up all that they had saved through an insurance scheme, would not get any pension and would have to turn to the Poor Law. Churchill was quite clear on this point, saying 'You qualify, we pay. If you do not qualify it is no good coming to us.' The Liberals believed that an insurance fund was welcome to workers who would feel they were taking back what they had earned: it was also a lot cheaper than simply paying money out of rates and taxes to help the unemployed. By 1914 there was a surplus of £23 millions in the insurance fund that was first set up in 1911.

To the House of Commons Churchill explained his very limited proposals:

Workmen coming to see what jobs are available at one of the very first labour exchanges at Camberwell, in February 1910. Notice how differently the clerks behind the counter are dressed. They were part of the growing number of officials needed to make the welfare state work.

'Our insurance scheme will involve contributions from the workpeople and from the employers, these contributions will be added to by the State. To what trades ought we as a beginning to apply our system of compulsory contributory unemployment insurance? They are trades in which seasonal unemployment is not only high, but chronic, marked by seasonal fluctuations; housebuilding and works of construction, engineering, machine and tool making, ship and boat building, sawyers and general labourers working at these trades. They comprise $2\frac{1}{4}$ million workers. We propose to follow the German example of insurance cards to which stamps will be affixed each week.'

Churchill defended the scheme as providing a lifebelt for those in temporary trouble; it did not cope with the long-term unemployed and it left out many occupations where there was short-term unemployment. Beveridge hoped that even more would be done. He wished to see the school leaving age raised to fifteen and the bringing in of a vigorous programme to train the young for suitable jobs in industry, but for the moment his bigger schemes had to wait.

KEY STEP: **The 1911 Insurance Act. Unemployment benefit**
Weekly contributions   from the employer $2\frac{1}{2}$d
                       from the employee $2\frac{1}{2}$d
                       from the state $1\frac{2}{3}$d
Benefit   7s a week for up to 15 weeks on the basis of one
          week's benefit for every five weeks contributions.
          No extra payments for dependants.

Health insurance

Churchill's scheme formed one part of the Insurance Act of 1911. Ill health cost many workers their jobs, and sometimes their lives too. Tuberculosis, for instance, claimed 75,000 lives a year; one of the victims had been Lloyd George's father. There were insurance companies that provided a means for workers to save privately, and indeed about six million people took advantage of them. But they were not always well-run organisations that working men could trust; moreover, as Lloyd George argued in 1909, 'There is a margin of people who cannot be persuaded or cannot afford systematic contributions. No plan can hope to be really comprehensive which

does not include an element of compulsion.' The organisations that already ran private schemes fiercely opposed the Chancellor's plans. Lloyd George complained about

'the bitter hostility of powerful organisations like the Prudential, the Pearl, and similar institutions with an army numbering scores if not hundreds of thousands of agents and collectors who make a living out of collecting a few pence a week from millions of households; a Government which attempted to take over their work without first of all securing the co-operation of the other party, would inevitably fail.'

These organisations were won round only when Lloyd George agreed to use them within the state scheme and to drop parts of his plan so that not too much of the business of private companies was menaced. The pensions that were to be paid to widows and orphans were dropped. This concession the Chancellor found especially difficult to make.

The scheme was administered by the big private companies who had been battling with Lloyd George, but was supervised by the state. The scheme did not provide hospital care, nor did it do anything for the insured workers' families.

The bill did not pass through parliament easily. Keir Hardie, the Labour leader, told South Wales miners that the government was saying 'We will not uproot the cause of poverty, but we will give you a porous plaster to cover the disease that poverty causes.' The Conservative Party, angry at the recent reduction in the power of the House of Lords, delayed it as far as they were able. There were attacks on it in the press and at public meetings where well-to-do ladies complained of having to lick stamps to stick on their servants' insurance cards.

The health insurance scheme meant that fewer people

KEY STEP: **The 1911 Insurance Act. Sickness Benefits**
Payments   4d a week from workers earning under £160 a
           year
           3d a week from employers
           2d a week from the state
Benefits   10s a week when ill for 26 weeks; free medical
           treatment from a doctor chosen by a local
           Insurance Commission and paid a fee according
           to the number of free (or 'panel') patients he
           had
           30s maternity benefit for the birth of each child

---

would need to seek the help of the old Poor Law; the ill health of the wage earner that reduced families to poverty could be survived, if it did not last too long, without going to the workhouse. Though this measure had its limitations, when added on to all the other things that Liberals had done it made Archbishop Lang decide, in 1911, 'The nineteenth century was concerned with the creation of wealth, the twentieth century will be concerned with its distribution.' The Liberals had not only extended state aid to the needy, they had provided it in ways that people found far more acceptable than that offered by the Poor Law in 1834. School meals and medicals, old age pensions, labour exchanges, sickness and unemployment benefits all operated outside the Poor Law; if this path for welfare benefits was followed in the future, the result would be the death of the old Poor Law from sheer neglect.

Summary of Key Steps

1905 Liberal government.
1906 Sweeping election victory for Liberals.

Liberal reforms for children

1906 Education (Provision of Meals) Act. Local councils allowed to provide meals and help pay for them from rates.
1907 Education Act. Medical inspection of all children.
1908 Children Act. New rules protecting children.

1908 Labour Exchange Act

A national system was begun, though workers and employers were not compelled to use them.

Liberal laws to improve working conditions

1908 8-hour working day at the coal face for miners.
1909 Trade Boards Act. Controlled wages and working conditions in small workshop activities like tailoring.
1911 The Shop Act. Introduced a legal weekly half-day holiday.

1908 Old Age Pensions Act

1909 Royal Commission on the Poor's Report

The Majority Report wanted a more efficient system of caring for the poor through local authorities and insurance schemes with checks to make sure the poor deserved help.
The Minority Report wanted the state to take charge of caring for the poor, labour exchanges and other services to help the poor, and a living standard to be set below which no one was to be allowed to drop.

1909 Lloyd George's Budget

1911 National Insurance Act

Parliament Act ended power of Lords to stop reform.

3 The Great War

Damage caused by the war

The outbreak of the First World War in 1914 was greeted with dismay by a keen new Liberal MP, Dr Christopher Addison. 'When one thinks of all our schemes of social reform just set a-going', he complained, 'and of those for which plans had been made in this year's budget, we could weep.'

It was the war which now took up the time of ministers and MPs; other plans had to be put aside. Men, money and materials were poured into winning the war, other areas where these resources were needed had to be neglected. In 1914 there was a serious shortage of housing; by 1918 it had grown into a huge problem because of the virtual stoppage of house-building during the war. The war took the lives of three-quarters of a million British men, and wounded over one and a half million more. It ate up British finances turning a pre-war national debt of £650 million into a post-war burden of £7,500 million. The war badly upset British trade, for British shipping and British resources were needed to supply the war effort: customers abroad, neglected by Britain, turned elsewhere. Some began building up their own industries, others bought from industrial lands such as the USA and Japan. The profits Britain earned from services to the rest of the world, such as banking, insurance, and shipping ('invisible' earnings), dropped sharply because of the problems of wartime. Some of the country's investments in foreign lands had to be sold off to help to pay for the war. All these economic difficulties made it hard to find money for expensive welfare measures.

Like the Boer War, the Great War showed up weaknesses in British society that needed attention. Addison later pointed out that

'For years our attention has been drawn to the fact that we have in our elementary schools armies who are physically defective. Every year they go and lose themselves in the mass of the population. We forget them until suddenly some great national event occurs. In the war we saw hundreds of thousands of men who were physically unfit. It is just as much a source of national weakness in time of peace.'

In 1916 the government moved beyond trying to strengthen the army through volunteers alone. It introduced conscription, compelling all men of 18–40 into military service. There had not been time for Liberal pre-war reforms to make much impact on the nation's health and probably the conscripts included many in even poorer shape than volunteers eager to join up. Of every nine conscripts examined after 1916, four were totally unfit for service and two were fit only for supporting duties, not for joining fighting units.

Seebohm Rowntree, brought in as an adviser to the Lloyd George government, drew up in 1917 a letter to employers in which he argued that Britain's economic power, like her military power, required a healthy population. 'If you would have a permanently efficient worker', he wrote, 'you must have a good citizen, adequately paid, and well-developed in body and mind.'

The war at least ended unemployment, and reduced the numbers in the workhouses. People were needed to fill the jobs of men in the armed forces, though they often lost them at the end of the war. Not only the making of munitions, but also the increased steel, coal, and shipbuilding output provided jobs in wartime conditions. Once peace came there would be a sudden rise in unemployment as wartime needs and jobs linked to those needs disappeared.

For the Liberal Party that had done so much for social

Numbers in workhouses

1914   282,000 people in workhouses
1919   183,000 people in workhouses
1 January 1914   7,800 people spent the night in a workhouse
1 January 1919   1,100 were in casual wards of a workhouse

These women shifting coke at a Cambridge gas works in 1916 are carrying out tasks that had been done by men until the Great War drew them into the armed services. The war forced many people to change their lives and to think about changing British society.

welfare between 1906 and 1914 the Great War was a disaster. The peacetime Prime Minister, Asquith, seemed increasingly ineffective as a warleader. Yet he was determined to remain in office and reluctant to see big changes in the way his government was run. In 1916 he was swept aside by a man with more energy and imagination, a man ready to put winning the war before the Liberal principles to which Asquith clung – David Lloyd George. With Conservative backing Lloyd George remained as Prime Minister for the rest of the war, but only at the cost of a growing gulf between his group of Liberals and the rest of the Party who still followed Asquith. The war left Liberals so split that they were never again able to form a government of their own.

The encouragement of reform

Britain had entered the war hopeful that it would soon end in victory. But as fighting continued with increasing savagery, as men were killed or crippled in such numbers that every town and nearly every village in Britain felt personally affected, so a change in mood came over the country. From the trade

unions, from Labour and some Liberal MPs, and from all sorts of private citizens came pressure to plan for a better post-war world so that the terrible war would not seem in vain.

Lloyd George was ready to respond to this mood. In the last year of the war he set up the Ministry of Reconstruction and made speeches promising a much-changed Britain. In doing this he was also trying to maintain his reputation as a reformer. Christopher Addison, the disappointed MP of 1914, became Minister of Reconstruction. As Addison explained, 'Reconstruction is not a question of rebuilding society as it was before the war, but of moulding a better world out of the social and economic conditions which have come into being during the war.'

Though the Liberal Party was now badly split, the Labour Party had, by the end of the war, developed into a more formidable force. It benefited from the fact that the government had needed to mobilise the whole of society to win the war. Trade union leaders found themselves given important jobs and some Labour men were taken into the government. Asquith had given but minor posts to Labour men but, for a while, the Labour leader Arthur Henderson served in Lloyd George's Cabinet. Trade union membership rose from 4 million in 1914 to 6 million in 1918. All these developments gave the Labour Party the confidence to strike out on its own. In 1918 it decided to fight the next election as an independent

Christopher Addison. 1869–1951. Qualified doctor who rose to become Professor of Anatomy at Sheffield University. Elected Liberal M.P. 1910 and served in several junior jobs before becoming Britain's first Minister of Health, 1919. Resigned in 1921 after quarrel with Lloyd George over ending of his chief project, the building of state-subsidised council houses. Joined Labour Party and became Minister of Agriculture (1929) and Dominions Secretary (1945).

body. It built up a national organisation, under Arthur Henderson's guidance, and it welcomed back into the party the minority who, led by Ramsay MacDonald, had split away in 1914 arguing that the Great War was wrong.

The Labour Party was openly committed to social reforms and wanted state power to be extended to make such reforms possible. At its 1918 conference it resolved

'This conference declares that the organisation and development of a unified health service for the whole community are questions of urgent importance and that steps should be taken without delay to establish a Ministry of Health based upon public health services and entirely disassociated from any Poor Law taints. The Public Health Acts should be extended so as to include within their scope all those duties now so inadequately provided under the Poor Law.'

Greater government power

The huge scale of the Great War had forced the government to take more and more power for itself. New ministries had been set up, such as the Ministry of Food and the Ministry of Shipping, to cope with wartime problems. By 1918 such essential foods as meat, sugar and butter were rationed. Taxes were increased, the running of railways and coal mines was now directed by the government, even the hours when public houses were open were strictly limited by the law in the belief that drunkenness was hampering the country's war effort.

Thus, by 1918, the state had greater powers and greater revenues than ever before. This gave it the chance to carry out big welfare reforms. Moreover in 1918 the government had rewarded the whole population for its war effort by giving the vote to all men over 21 and women over 30. It was likely that this mass of ordinary voters would insist that their MPs pass welfare reforms.

Some reforms had already come into being during 1918. They included a new Education Act that scrapped the fees charged in elementary schools, insisted on fourteen as the minimum school leaving age, planned better schooling opportunities for those over 14, and promised better pay for teachers. In 1916 the government widened the 1911 Insurance Act to include far more workers.

ROYAL PROCLAMATION
YOU ARE ASKED TO REDUCE YOUR CONSUMPTION OF BREAD BY ¼

THE PRICE OF VICTORY.
WELL, OLD GIRL, IF WE CAN'T DO THAT MUCH, WE DON'T DESERVE TO WIN.

This 'Punch' cartoon shows how the government at first asked people to cut consumption. When this failed they introduced rationing. Similarly, private social help has gradually given place to the compulsory welfare state.

In 1917 and 1918 discontent with the war led to workers' revolutions in Russia and Germany. Alarmed that the same might happen in Britain, the government tried to stave off trouble. In 1918 it created a serious breach in the insurance principle. Ex-service people and ex-war workers were provided with an 'out-of-work donation' whether or not they had

This children's party in London's East End is one of thousands held to celebrate the end of the terrible Great War, when every-one looked forward to a better life and more peaceful world. The street is decorated with the flags of Britain and her allies, including Japan and USA.

been paying contributions as part of the insurance scheme. Another important change was that extra allowances were given for families. 29s a week could be drawn for up to 20 weeks, 6s was added for the first child and 3s for each additional child. In this way ministers hoped to provide people with enough to get by on whilst they moved back to civilian life and found fresh work.

During 1918 Addison was busy planning the setting up of a brand-new Ministry of Health (though he had to wait till the following year before his new responsibility was officially born). He intended to tackle the housing shortage as his first priority and then to look carefully at ways of improving the health services available to the public.

The Great War ended in a surge of hope. Though thousands had died and the war had hurt Britain's economic strength, it seemed also to have altered the political mood in the country. Lloyd George believed, in 1918, 'the whole state of society is more or less molten. The country will be prepared for bigger things immediately after the war.' With the Prime Minister himself fighting the 1918 election campaign on the platform of building 'a land fit for heroes', it seemed reasonable for many to regard the terrible experience of the Great War as an event that could produce some more positive results. Moreover fear of post-war trouble if reforms were not carried out, further encouraged government actions.

4 The troubled twenties

Post-war plans

A general election in late 1918 confirmed Lloyd George as Prime Minister. The massive majority was made up of Conservatives, in a union, or coalition, with those Liberals who followed Lloyd George rather than Asquith. For the moment Conservative leaders admired Lloyd George for leading Britain to victory in the Great War, and felt his leadership was still needed to tackle post-war problems. The Conservative leader, Andrew Bonar Law, had agreed with Lloyd George on policies that were set out in an election manifesto in November 1918. The two leaders stated that:

'One of the first tasks of the Government will be to deal on broad and comprehensive lines with the housing of the people which during the war has fallen so sadly into arrears. Larger opportunities for education, improved material conditions, and the prevention of degrading standards of employment, these are among the conditions of social harmony which we will earnestly endeavour to promote.'

But the end of the Great War had come more suddenly than politicians had expected. Peacetime plans were far from fully prepared and the country did not seem ready to wait patiently for gradual changes. There were strikes, marches, and demonstrations in 1919–20 affecting large groups of workers and even army units who felt that demobilisation was going too slowly. The government was pressed by businessmen to start as soon as possible to cut controls and taxation and get back to pre-war conditions. It was therefore difficult to draw up plans in a calm and careful way and to be confident that the government would have the power and the money to carry out those plans.

At the new Ministry of Health Christopher Addison busied himself with plans for providing Britain with sufficient housing. He ordered local authorities to survey their areas and report their housing needs to him. Addison then urged them to start building houses to be rented, and to pay for them out of the rates. Where the income from the rates was not sufficient, the extra cost would be borne by the government. By the time the Coalition ended in 1922 110,000 houses had been completed under this scheme.

At the end of the war the Unemployment Insurance Fund had a surplus of £21 million. Though ministers knew that switching from war to peace would mean a time of unemployment, they did not expect this to last long and had provided the 'out-of-work donation' to deal with it. It seemed, therefore, safe enough to widen the 1911 insurance scheme to embrace more groups of workers. From 1920 all workers earning up to £5 a week were brought into the scheme, save those employed in agriculture, the civil service and domestic service. The rate of benefit was now fixed at 15s a week.

The coming of depression

From 1920 the government had to face increasingly strong signs that unemployment was not going to be a brief post-war experience. The damage done by the war to Britain's economy was not the only reason for a sluggish level of business activity which resulted in many workers losing their jobs. Peacetime Britain was too dependent on old-fashioned industries like textiles, coal, and shipbuilding. There were too few jobs in the newer industries of electrical goods, chemicals, and vehicle

The 1918 election

339	Coalition Conservatives
44	Other Conservatives
136	Coalition Liberals
26	Asquith Liberals
59	Labour

building. The older industries depended very heavily on exports, and by the twenties were being vigorously challenged by more efficient rivals in other lands. The inevitable result was unemployment. A Labour leader told a meeting, in December 1920, 'There was not a more pathetic spectacle than the unemployed victims of our social order. They include a large number of men who a few years ago were priceless heroes, but who were now "worthless wasters".'

A group of people investigating health in Manchester reported, in 1922, 'The physique of a great number of workers is undoubtedly being impaired by prolonged unemployment. That the majority of the unemployed are disheartened and miserable and feel utterly helpless and insecure there can be no doubt.'

Numbers of insured workers unemployed

1921	2,038,000
1924	1,263,000
1929	1,344,000

Government cuts

Ministers could see only one answer to the problem of rising unemployment and a poor economic performance. They believed they must cut government spending and reduce government controls over the economy; this would help them to keep taxes down. They hoped that trade would gradually revive and Lloyd George sought to bring this about by organising conferences where European states tried to sort out their differences. The Prime Minister was not successful; the strong feelings between France and Germany were especially hard to overcome. Yet the government had little else it could do; there was no powerful well-argued case for a different policy. When Labour MPs criticised the government it was in vague terms; they argued that the whole way British society was organised was wrong but could think of little to be done in detail, here and now.

So the government handed back the mines and railways to private owners, rejecting a report in favour of nationalising the coal industry. One of the first victims of the search for cuts in spending was the housing programme. By 1921 Addison's scheme was costing the Treasury £12 million and the minister was blamed for having planned his scheme badly. The

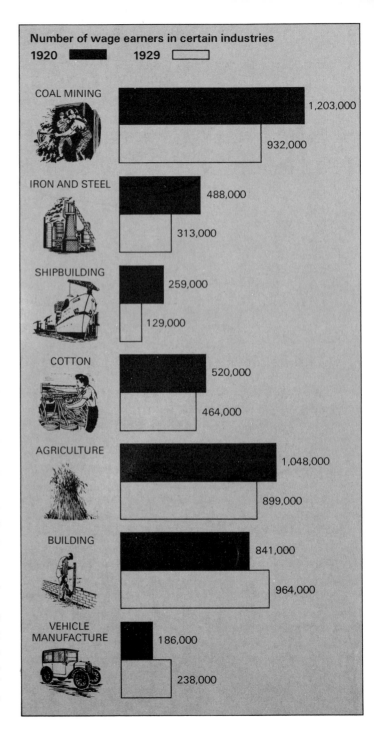

Number of wage earners in certain industries
1920 ■   1929 □

COAL MINING — 1,203,000 / 932,000

IRON AND STEEL — 488,000 / 313,000

SHIPBUILDING — 259,000 / 129,000

COTTON — 520,000 / 464,000

AGRICULTURE — 1,048,000 / 899,000

BUILDING — 841,000 / 964,000

VEHICLE MANUFACTURE — 186,000 / 238,000

Treasury support for house-building was stopped, Addison was dismissed, and showed his feelings by going to join a small group of ex-Liberals now in the Labour Party. Part of the 1918 Education Act – the setting up of schools for part-time education for those over 14 – was scrapped and teachers' salaries were cut as part of a general reduction in the wages of government servants.

So many people were out of work that the insurance fund ran into debt. In desperation, the government was forced to start paying 'uncovenanted' benefits, that is payments to unemployed people who had used up all the benefits they were entitled to under the Insurance Act. The alternative was to force all the unemployed who had used up their brief weeks of rightfully earned payments onto the Poor Law. The out-of-work were not evenly spread over the country but concentrated in areas where jobs were largely found in coalmining or shipbuilding. Poor Law guardians in these areas would have been swamped if all long-term unemployed people had to turn to them.

The government still hoped, in 1921 and 1922, that it was dealing with a situation that would not last. The uncovenanted benefits paid were regarded as advances on future contributions by the people receiving them. In 1921 allowances for dependents were conceded to the unemployed at the rate of 5s a week for a wife and 1s for each child. This meant a family of five would have 23s a week, yet Professor A. L. Bowley, an expert on food whom the government itself used in enquiries, believed that such a family needed at least £2 a week for food alone, and £3 13s 6d for all their requirements. Families that had to go month after month without a wage were forced to borrow, to sell precious possessions and, in the end, to turn to the Poor Law for extra help.

Numbers on Poor Relief

January 1921	750,000
July 1922	2,000,000

Poplarism

Both people for whom unemployment benefits were insufficient, and people outside insurance schemes sought help from the Poor Law guardians. Under this pressure, the guardians reacted in different ways. In some areas they began

Weekly diet for family of 5 allowed by Birmingham Poor Law guardians through a system of food vouchers

Tea	9 oz	Cheese or bacon	1¾ lb
Sugar	3½ lb	Condensed milk	2 14-oz tins
Rice or sago	12 oz	Margarine or lard	2 lb
Rolled oats or dried fruit	2 lb	Cocoa	8 oz
Golden syrup	2 lb	Soap	1 lb
Split peas	1½ lb	Bread	22 lb
Plain flour	2½ lb		

to ignore the rules about how able-bodied men should be treated. Instead of offering them a workhouse place or an eight-hour stone-breaking job in a labour yard, they supplied food vouchers.

No guardians went further in breaking the rules than the Labour guardians of the London East End Poplar area. They paid generous scales of relief, ran into debt, and then refused to hand over to London County Council payments they were supposed to make. For six weeks in 1921 the guardians were imprisoned, yet refused to give way, and eventually triumphed. All London areas shared the costs of poor relief in future so that Poplar did not have to carry an unduly heavy burden. Yet still they gave trouble, paying £2 19s 6d to a family of seven instead of £2 14s (the agreed London rate). In families with more than five children, they paid 5s for every extra child. The result was that an out-of-work family that was very large could receive a bigger income in poor relief than if the husband were earning wages in the local docks.

The Poplar guardians handed out clothing far more readily than was thought proper, and allowed a diet in the workhouse that government officials regarded as far too generous. Officials especially disapproved of the inmates receiving butter instead of margarine. But the Poplar guardians defended their readiness to pay generously, declaring, 'There is no crying or whining on the part of those who apply for

Diet in the Poplar Workhouse, 1922

Breakfast:	Tea, bread (3 oz), butter (½ oz), porridge (¾ pint), milk (¼ pint)
Dinner:	meat (or fish, or meat pudding) (3 oz), rice or treacle pudding (4 oz)
Tea:	bread (6–8 oz), tea (1 pint), butter (½ oz), cake or jam or cured fish or cheese

A demonstration in 1921 in favour of Poplar's Labour borough council.

public assistance.' Further punishment might well have fallen upon them but for the distraction of three general elections between 1922 and 1924.

The 1923 Housing Act

In 1922 the Coalition collapsed. Most Conservatives now felt their party no longer needed Lloyd George and his Coalition Liberals. The election that followed proved them right. A Conservative Ministry was elected in which the key post of Minister of Health was, from March 1923, held by Neville Chamberlain. Chamberlain already had vast experience in local government having risen to the post of Lord Mayor of Birmingham. He was one of the most thorough and hard-working ministers during the inter-war years with a keen interest in reforms that would end muddle and uncertainty. His rather harsh public manner tended to hide his very real concern for social reforms. In 1923 he tackled the housing problem that had broken Addison's Liberal career. Treasury money at the rate of £6 per house for twenty years was offered to private house-builders, Chamberlain hoped that this would

Neville Chamberlain. 1869–1940. Member of wealthy Birmingham industrial family and son of politician Joseph Chamberlain. Lord Mayor of Birmingham 1915–16. Chancellor of Exchequer 1923–4 and 1931–7, Minister of Health 1924–9, Prime Minister 1937–40. A very hard working minister, eager to see efficient government and responsible for some of the main inter-war policies of house-building, reform of the Poor Law and reform of Local Government. Forced to concentrate on foreign affairs, he proved a failure in this field. A man who seemed cold and distant, a skilful and often sarcastic speaker.

encourage better-off families to move to new houses, leaving older houses for less well-off families to occupy. Councils, Chamberlain decided, were simply to provide homes for poorer people for whom no private contractor was prepared to build.

Labour in office, 1924

In December 1923 Stanley Baldwin, leader of the Conservative government, called an election. Although it was only a year since there had been an election, Baldwin decided a new one was needed to see if people would support a change in policy that he was proposing. He had concluded that by taxing many of the goods imported into Britain, the government would make it easier for British manufacturers to out-sell their foreign rivals in their home market. This should reduce unemployment in Britain.

But voters chose a majority of Liberal and Labour MPs, who still supported free trade, and Baldwin resigned. A Labour government was formed, though it needed Liberal votes to keep it in power. The new ministers were deeply concerned about problems of poverty and unemployment yet they had no new policies to offer to transform the situation. Any scheme that needed a great deal of money from the

Treasury was bound to fail for the new Chancellor of the Exchequer, Philip Snowden, was a firm believer in free trade and as low a level of taxation as possible. The Prime Minister, Ramsay MacDonald, tried (as Lloyd George had done) to help Britain's economy to revive by working at improving the prospects of long-term world peace. He had some success in this respect, yet little benefit seemed to come to Britain's declining exports.

Labour policies concentrated on making the existing system less harsh. They increased the money paid to the unemployed; they scrapped the system of having gaps of several weeks when nothing was given to the unemployed, between periods when payments were made. Their Health Minister, John Wheatley, launched a new house-building programme. He offered local authorities £9 a year for each house for up to 40 years if they

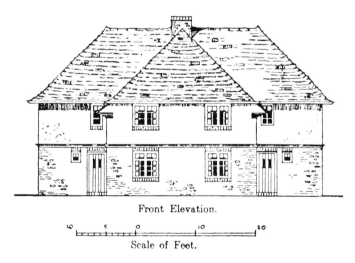

Front Elevation.

Scale of Feet.

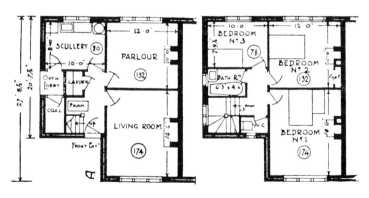

Ground Floor Plan.   First Floor Plan.

Plan and elevation of three-bedroom semi-detached houses designed by the Ministry of Health in the 1920s for local authorities to build. The living room is 4.4 m × 3.7 m (14 ft 6 in × 12 ft).

27

would build council houses. This abolished Chamberlain's attempt to restrict local authority house-building to providing for those for whom no private builder would act. Yet even these council houses were too dear for many working people. In Blackburn three-bedroomed properties offered at rents between 17s 4d and 18s 2d a week attracted not one applicant: two-bedroomed homes at 10s 6d to 12s 4d were more popular. An unemployed family of four now getting 27s a week after Labour's increases, still could not afford one of these new homes.

Houses built 1920–30	
by local authorities	611,012
by subsidised private building	423,447
by unsubsidised private building	584,912

Neville Chamberlain's reforms, 1924–9

Labour lost office in late 1924 when Liberals refused to continue supporting them and the electors chose a Conservative government. Neville Chamberlain returned to the Health Ministry, determined to bring in changes that would make several aspects of social policy work more smoothly.

In 1925 he altered the old age pension scheme. The original Liberal provision of pensions paid to people over 70, according to their income, remained, but to it Chamberlain added a new structure of pensions for the over 65s. This pension was paid without any means test, but it went only to those who had been paying the health insurance contributions for at least five years. Thus old age pensions for most people were gradually put on the same footing as sickness payments: they were earned by people paying a weekly 9d insurance stamp to which employers added a further ninepence.

The opportunity was also taken to introduce a 10s a week pension for widows, and 7s 6d for orphans. Though only those earning less than £250 benefited, most old people were now freed from the 'means test', by which officials checked on their living conditions and income before allowing payment.

In 1927 the government allowed unemployment payments to anyone who had made thirty insurance payments over their working life, or who had made at least eight payments in two years.

Then Chamberlain tackled the Poor Law. He thought it

wasteful, inefficient and confusing to have both local authorities and separate Poor Law guardians to deal with those in need. He disliked the way those at Poplar and elsewhere had been breaking the rules, and he realised that ratepayers in towns with much unemployment were carrying an unfair burden. So the guardians were abolished, and their duties were passed to the county councils and county boroughs, which dealt with larger areas. These local authorities set up new Public Assistance Committees, which provided help for the poor; but only after inspectors had checked that it was really needed.

Chamberlain's work was halted by the defeat of his government in the 1929 election. For the new Labour ministers who took over, even bigger problems of poverty began to loom up.

Summary of Key Steps

Post-war reconstruction

1918 Education Act. Fees in elementary schools were abolished. School leaving age raised to fourteen.

1919 Setting up of Ministry of Health to supervise housing, health, the poor and insurance schemes. State help to encourage council house-building till 1921.

1920 Insurance Act. Insurance against unemployment extended to include more jobs.

1924 Housing Act

Labour scheme to encourage council house-building with Treasury help.

Chamberlain's reforms

1923 Housing Act. State help to encourage private house-building.

1925 Old Age Pensions. Additional scheme added for pensions for over 65s without means test but depending on insurance contributions.

1929 Local Government Act. Bigger local authorities took over the duties of the Poor Law guardians.

5 The slump

The new Labour government

In 1929 Ramsay MacDonald once again led a Labour government. Only one party had offered vigorous detailed policies to the voters, the Liberals, led by Lloyd George. The Liberal claim 'We can Conquer Unemployment' was based on ideas that had been worked out over several years by groups of experts. Lloyd George tried to convince the voters that by spending far more government money (raised from higher taxes and from borrowing) jobs could be created and declining industries revived. But only 59 Liberals were elected. Perhaps voters distrusted Lloyd George.

Labour, however, was not well prepared to tackle unemployment. Snowden was as opposed to large-scale government spending as he had ever been. The government had 288 MPs, the Conservatives 260, which left the government without a clear working majority. But this does not seem to have stopped ministers acting boldly. Their answer to unemployment was to make the existing system work a little more generously.

There were men within Labour's ranks who were ready to offer new policies. In 1930 one of the Party's junior ministers, Oswald Mosley, produced his solution in a 'Memorandum'. He suggested that by taxing imports, getting government control of the banks, paying higher pensions and helping industry reorganise with state money, Britain could be transformed. His Party rejected the scheme and in despair Mosley left it and set up his own New Party.

Instead Labour continued with well-tried policies: making unemployment benefits more generous and tackling another aspect of Britain's housing problem. In 1930 the rule that people claiming unemployment benefits must show that they were genuinely seeking work was dropped. At the Health Ministry Arthur Greenwood was alert to housing evidence, like that offered by Manchester's Lord Mayor in 1929, who said, 'We have done nothing for the poorer workers. The condition of the slums in which they are forced to live is probably worse today than it was at the end of the war. Overcrowding is almost certainly no less.' Plenty of investigators reported houses like this Manchester home: 'Number 6 is a one up and one down house. It is damp and very verminous. The family consists of husband, wife, sons aged 19, 14, 7, 1, and daughters 17, 11 and 5.'

Greenwood drew up a Housing Act to begin clearing slums and replacing them with decent homes that poorer people could afford. But his scheme had to wait four years before it could really begin because Britain became involved in a world crisis that wrecked the Labour government.

The world slump

From 1929 a slump in world trade that started in the USA, spread across much of the globe. The boom enjoyed by many lands (though not Britain) in the later twenties had depended far too much on borrowed money. In 1929 confidence in businesses and banks began to collapse. As banks and companies failed, trade slumped, unemployment rose and Americans called in the money they had been lending abroad, money that had done much to prevent depression in Europe. It was reckoned that by the middle of 1930 the number of unemployed in 33 countries had doubled in a year.

The slump hit Europe in 1931. The failure of the Vienna Bank was followed by financial and business failures across the continent. Many countries tried to protect their struggling industries by increasing taxes on imports. World trade was made even more difficult for exporting countries like Britain by the troubles of countries producing food and raw materials. These 'primary' producers found that they were marketing more than they could sell; their earnings were therefore dropping, and they had less money to pay for imports.

Workers in Britain registered as unemployed

| | 1930 | 1931 | 1932 | 1933 | 1934 | 1935 | 1936 | 1937 | 1938 |

Average earnings in shillings a week

1931 ■

1935 □

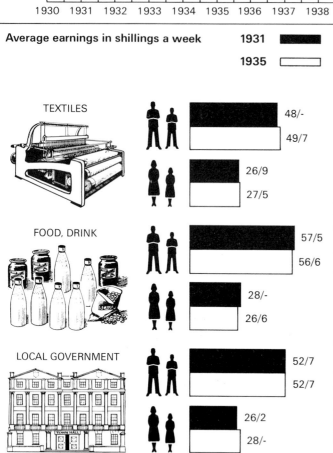

TEXTILES

48/-
49/7

26/9
27/5

FOOD, DRINK

57/5
56/6

28/-
26/6

LOCAL GOVERNMENT

52/7
52/7

26/2
28/-

The percentage of people out of work in certain jobs

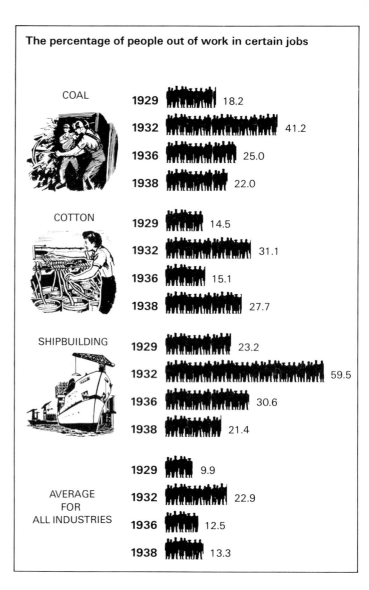

COAL

1929 18.2
1932 41.2
1936 25.0
1938 22.0

COTTON

1929 14.5
1932 31.1
1936 15.1
1938 27.7

SHIPBUILDING

1929 23.2
1932 59.5
1936 30.6
1938 21.4

AVERAGE FOR ALL INDUSTRIES

1929 9.9
1932 22.9
1936 12.5
1938 13.3

For Britain the world slump meant that industries depending heavily on exports suffered a loss of business that threw yet more of their workers out of employment. It also meant that the world's financial problems spread to Britain's banks too. But the cost of imports into Britain also fell and the slump brought advantages to those who could keep their jobs because the cost of living dropped by about a third.

The number of unemployed insured workers (as a percentage of all insured workers)

London and S.E. England, Midlands, Northern England, Wales, Scotland

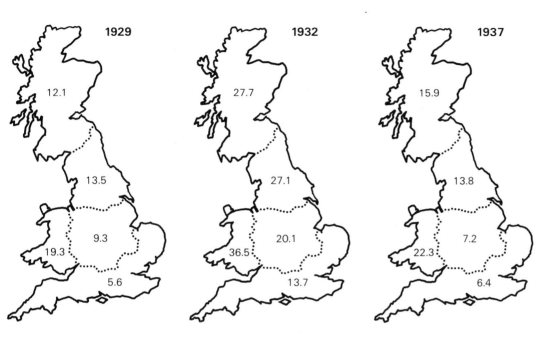

1929
12.1
13.5
9.3
19.3
5.6

1932
27.7
27.1
20.1
36.5
13.7

1937
15.9
13.8
7.2
22.3
6.4

The crisis of 1931

MacDonald appointed a committee under Sir George May's leadership to advise the government how best to act. The May Report appeared on 31 July 1931. It stated that the government was spending far too much money and suggested cuts in the wages of people who worked for the government. The biggest cut recommended was a 20% reduction in the money paid to the unemployed. The Cabinet split over the question of cuts in unemployment benefits. Trade union leaders furiously opposed the reductions and some Labour men felt them quite unacceptable. MacDonald led a small minority who were

The May Report

Taxes to be increased by £24 millions a year
Cuts in spending on wages and salaries totalling £29½ millions
Cuts in unemployment benefit of £66½ millions

ready to stay in a new Coalition 'National Government' to cope with the crisis: the bulk of the Labour Party withdrew from government and, not long afterwards, expelled the people who had once led them but whom they now saw as traitors. The newly formed government cut the weekly payments to the unemployed, a man's money from 17s to 15s 3d and a wife's from 9s to 8s. These payments were made for 26 weeks, then anyone still needing help had to accept an investigation into all they owned carried out by local authority officials. After this 'means test', a level of payment was decided that might well be lower than that paid for the 26 week insurance period. A general election in October 1931 in which MacDonald appealed for 'a doctor's mandate' to tackle unemployment produced 556 Coalition MPs.

The Labour Party had not been able to do a great deal for social welfare from 1929 to 1931. It shrank from spending huge amounts on trying to create new jobs; it would not put

31

above: *Unemployed men queuing at a labour exchange in 1925.*

right: *Alfred Smith, unemployed in 1939, gives his wife the week's housekeeping money. Unemployment benefit was £2 7s 6d a week.*

high taxes on imports to protect jobs in Britain. But Britain did not suffer as badly as many other lands in the Great Depression and the money paid to those out of work was generous by world standards. The Labour Party gradually recovered from the crisis and began to win back votes. In lands where the slump was more severe there was far more political trouble than in Britain.

The National Government

The British economy began to slowly recover from the crisis of 1931. As business picked up again so the numbers of those without jobs fell to levels more like those of the twenties. The

Growing numbers in certain jobs	1929	1938
BUILDING	742,000	906,000
ELECTRICAL TRADES	185,000	312,000
BUILDING AND MENDING VEHICLES, CYCLES, AIRCRAFT	228,000	355,000
PRINTING AND PUBLISHING	257,000	265,000

government helped this recovery in various ways. It taxed many imports into Britain in order to help British farming and British industries. It negotiated with Commonwealth countries in order to increase trade. It made it easier for people to borrow money at low rates of interest. Small amounts of money were spent to encourage depressed industries to modernise. Lloyd George was sceptical about the small amount of money allowed to the Commissioners for creating work in depressed areas. 'The age of miracles is past', he said. 'You cannot feed the multitude with two Commissioners and five sub-Commissioners. The new Commissioners are being sent on their apostolic mission – not without purse and scrip – but very nearly that – just a little bit of money.'

By 1934 the government felt secure enough to start to undo some of its earlier restrictions. The unemployed were freed from the cuts of 1931 and Greenwood's slum-clearance policies were now put into operation. At the centre of financial and social policy-making was Neville Chamberlain. He served as Minister of Health, then (November 1931) as Chancellor of the Exchequer and finally as Prime Minister. In 1934 Chamberlain produced another plan to reform unemployment benefits. He was especially concerned that the local authorities, who examined people applying for help after their 26 weeks of payments were used, behaved differently in different parts of Britain. The Rotherham authority seemed to the government so generous that, in 1932, its officials who dealt with the unemployed were dismissed and replaced by a government commissioner.

Chamberlain wanted to see a national system for dealing with the unemployed. He set up an Unemployment Assistance Board that dealt with all unemployed people who had used their 26 weeks of payments. The money paid out by the Board came from the Treasury, not from local rates. When the Board made known the rates it would pay (24s for a married couple compared with 26s for people getting the 26-weeks worth of insurance payments) there was such an outcry from places where local authorities had been paying more that the scheme had to be brought in gradually over the years 1934 to 1937.

Better care for babies

By the 1936 Midwives Act local authorities were required to provide trained personnel.
By 1938 there were 1,795 ante-natal clinics in England and Wales. Some areas had Welfare Centres and provided free or cheap milk to expectant mothers.

Life on the dole

A visitor in the 1930s to one of Britain's slump towns, Merthyr in Wales, remembered being 'amazed by the number of people there in it. The street was simply crowded. The extraordinary thing is that the people were not doing anything, they were not moving, it was as if they were turned to stone, and I suddenly realised that this was what went on every day in Merthyr.'

In places where many people went months, even years,

without work, life was monotonous. The men had little to do once their unemployment pay, commonly called 'the dole', had been collected. In Wigan the writer George Orwell described an unemployed man: 'He was standing there as motionless as a statue, cap neb pulled over his eyes, gaze fixed on the pavement, hands in pockets, shoulders hunched, the bitter wind blowing his thin trousers against his legs. Waste paper and dust blew about him.'

Managing on the dole threw great strain on the woman in a household. 24s a week was the level of the dole for a married couple after 1934, plus extra allowances for children. This is how a Greenock man, his wife, and eight children spent their weekly payment of £1 19s 3d.

Rent	12s	Potatoes	2s		Vegetables	11d
Gas	3s	Margarine	1s		Rice	4d
Societies	1s 4d	Tea		9d	Dripping	3d
Coal	2s 3d	Sugar		10d	Tea-bread	6d
Milk	2s 4d	Bread	7s		Fish	10d
Soap	8d	Meat	2s	10d	Biscuits	4d
					Salt and pepper	1d

The dole was only given after families had been checked to see if they had money of their own or other sources of income. Whether this was done by local authorities before 1934 or the Unemployment Assistance Board after 1934, it was strongly disliked. Children who earned a few shillings found that this amount would be knocked off their father's dole: a war-widow's pension or an old age pension could be reasons for cutting a family's payments. Until 1934 the dole might be cut off if officials found that a family had any savings; after that date they were allowed up to £200 of savings. The means test encouraged the break-up of families where one of the younger members had a job that led officials to cut the dole paid the father of the household. Investigators working for the Carnegie Trust thought that 'weakening of family solidarity and

Number of registered vehicles (private cars, commercial vehicles, buses)

1931	1,076,128	348,969	86,208
1935	1,455,721	414,760	85,223
1938	1,916,226	471,156	87,536

disintegration of home life is perhaps the most serious and challenging aspect of the means test. The realisation that every cigarette smoked is paid for by the sacrifice of a brother or sister arouses bitterness, not against the regulations, but rather against the brother or sister who is fortunate enough to be able to help.'

Investigators found that people living in areas of high unemployment were more likely to be ill than those in better-off regions. Some ailments sprang from a poor diet, some from the mental depression of years of struggling to live on the dole. For people who were ill, the inter-war years saw little improvement. The 1911 health insurance scheme did not give the dependants of the insured worker any right to free treatment; it still applied. Fees for dentists and opticians were too high for the poor. Thus people in the depressed areas were more likely to be ill and less likely to get proper treatment.

The government had done enough to prevent people living on the dole from starving to death. It did not believe it should spend more money partly because the country could not afford it and partly because it thought people would be deterred from genuinely seeking work if their dole were generous. But men who had lost their jobs lost their dignity too. A. M. Cameron described how such a man felt. 'He is ashamed of his lapse from higher standards but the shame only depresses him the more. He wanders about with no end in view, a ghost among living men.'

A better life

In 1934 the writer J. B. Priestley toured Britain. He went to the depressed regions, to the farmlands, and also to 'the England of arterial and by-pass roads, of filling stations and factories that look like exhibition buildings, of giant cinemas and dance halls and cafés, bungalows with tiny garages, cocktail bars, Woolworths, motor coaches, wireless, hiking, factory girls looking like actresses, greyhound racing and dirt tracks, swimming pools and everything given away for cigarette coupons.' Government struggles to create welfare systems to help those in trouble should be seen against an inter-war background of greater prosperity for the majority of people. Those in steady work were greatly helped by the fall in the cost of living, by the mass-production methods that made so many goods available to them, and by arrangements (like those made by building societies) that helped them borrow money cheaply.

Signs of affluence

1925–39	A four-fold increase in electricity consumption.
1931–5	Marks and Spencers opened 129 new stores.
1930s	Average mortgage interest rate, 4½%.
	Cost of typical 3 bedroomed semi-detached house, £450.
1937	Butlin's first holiday camp at Skegness.
1914–34	Increased consumption of some foods: fruit 88%, vegetables 64%, eggs 46%.

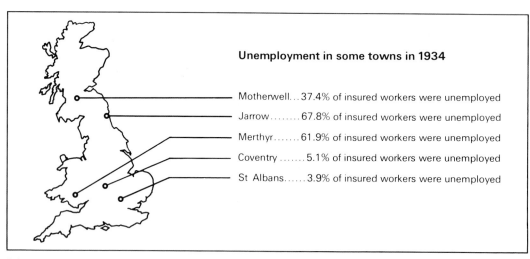

Unemployment in some towns in 1934

Motherwell…37.4% of insured workers were unemployed

Jarrow……..67.8% of insured workers were unemployed

Merthyr…….61.9% of insured workers were unemployed

Coventry …….5.1% of insured workers were unemployed

St Albans……3.9% of insured workers were unemployed

People with jobs were usually better off in the thirties since the cost of many goods fell. Many were able to buy or rent homes, and there was a growing demand for furniture and electrical goods. This 1936 White City exhibition shows the latest fashionable furnishings. Industries supplying goods of this kind naturally grew up in the south of England, where most of the customers lived. The government made some efforts to encourage such industries in the regions of highest unemployment.

The results could be seen throughout the country but were especially noticeable in the Midlands and South East where there were plenty of jobs in expanding industries. More people could afford private homes, while within the homes were more elaborate furnishings and electrical gadgets than ever before. The holiday business expanded, by 1939 eleven million workers enjoyed holidays with pay. There was a growth of cinema building (4,700 were open by 1937) and other leisure activities, such as soccer, tennis, greyhound racing, newspaper reading, all became more popular. Seebohm Rowntree recognised these improvements when, in 1936, he made another study of York and found that those living in poverty were half as numerous as in 1899. He found three reasons for this:

'The first is the reduction in the size of family: the second is the increase in real wages. The third cause is the remarkable growth of social services in the period. Great though the progress made has been, there is no cause for satisfaction in the fact that in a country so rich as England over 30% of the workers in a typical provincial city should have incomes so small that it is beyond their means to live even at a stringently economical level.'

By 1939 the state was doing far more to help those in need than it had done in 1934. It had responded to a series of crises with policies that were not part of a carefully planned overall scheme. Many people in the 1930s thought that the state should do still more. They were busy drawing up reports and plans when the outbreak of another world war brought normal life to a halt.

Summary of Key Steps

1931 National Government cut unemployment pay and welfare services.

1934 Unemployment Act

Setting up of Unemployment Assistance Board to see that the out of work were paid according to a national scale and were paid from state not local funds.

6 The Second World War

The impact of war

It was soon clear to everyone that the Second World War was not going to be brief. Neville Chamberlain seemed so unsuited to wartime leadership that he was edged out of the Premiership by the mounting mutiny of his own Party. He remained in the Cabinet for a few months until his death in 1940. He was replaced by Winston Churchill. The government that Churchill created was meant to be truly national, representing Britain's determination to resist Hitler and Mussolini. So Churchill offered places in the Cabinet to members of the Labour Party, and they accepted. Labour's leader, Clement Attlee, became the Deputy Prime Minister and important posts also went to Herbert Morrison, Arthur Greenwood and Stafford Cripps. The post of Minister of Labour, vital for organising the manpower for the war effort at home, went to a Labour man who was not even an MP. This was Ernest Bevin, the formidable leader of the Transport and General Workers Union. His ability and his influence over the trade unions made Churchill decide he was the right man for this difficult job.

Churchill kept the direction of the war itself very much in his own hands, but Labour Party men helped to organise Britain for war and cope with the effects of German bomb attacks on Britain. In this indirect way the Party that had made social welfare such an important part of its programme could gain valuable experience of governing and influence what was done. The home front in the Second World War was a battlefield itself. German bombers flew over much of the country destroying factories, communications, military targets and people's homes. Many British ships were sunk by German submarines and surface raiders. The government had to plan very carefully to make the best use of the country's very limited home produced food and the even more limited quantities of essential goods that had eluded the German menace. The task of coping with this crisis was very much eased by the experience of the Great War upon which ministers could draw in designing their various schemes.

Winston Churchill. 1874–1965. Grandson of Duke and son of politician Lord Randolph Churchill. Educated at Harrow and Sandhurst. Adventurer, soldier, author and statesman who tackled problems with huge enthusiasm. Conservative M.P. 1900–5 and from 1924 but Liberal M.P. 1906–23. President of Board of Trade 1908–10 and introduced Labour Exchanges as well as strongly supporting Lloyd George's work, especially unemployment insurance. From 1911 more concerned with foreign, colonial and military matters. Prime Minister 1940–5 and 1951–5: concerned lest social reform use up too much money and weaken Britain as a world force.

The cost of war

300,000 armed service personnel killed. 60,000 civilians killed. 35,000 merchant seamen killed. 3½ million houses damaged or destroyed.

In 1939 and 1940 the railway stations of Britain's big cities were full of scenes like this. Fearful of German bombing, parents sent their children away to parts of the country that were thought to be safe. The children are labelled and carry gas masks.

The fear that German bombing would destroy many thousands of the population led the government to organise the moving of children from towns and cities that were likely to be attacked to more remote parts of the country. This mass evacuation separated children from their parents. A London bus driver remembered 'it was a pitiful sight to see so many thousands of small children, all labelled and carrying small cases and parcels. Some crying, some happy, all going to strange homes.' Many of these children came from slums. The condition of their health and clothing, their habits, their ignorance of baths and water closets, shocked their new hosts. 'Their clothing was in a deplorable condition', one lady exclaimed, 'some of the children being literally sewed into their ragged little garments. Except for a small number the children were filthy and we have never seen so many verminous children lacking any knowledge of clean and hygenic habits.'

It was not only evacuation that brought together sections of society who in peacetime had little to do with one another. The armed forces gathered together men from different classes; bombs fell on the rich as well as the poor; wartime industry attracted into it women who in peacetime might never have considered such work. Government controls affected the whole of the population. The rationing of food and clothing was soon in force and the government also standardised the quality and design of many goods to avoid waste. Conscription affected not only the younger male population, but also unmarried females. People were conscripted to serve in the armed forces, in essential industry (especially coal mining) and in farming.

The Second World War was enormously expensive. The government had to abandon its careful pre-war spending policy. It increased taxes and borrowed money from abroad to win the war. Churchill's expert advisers included the economist J. M. Keynes, who had tried to persuade ministers to tackle the slump by using the power of the state vigorously. Now he had the chance to influence government measures from the inside. Thus, in economic policy, as in politics and in everyday life, the Second World War had a huge impact on Britain.

Welfare reforms

Once more war highlighted some of the flaws in British society. The Ministry of Food planned the rationing scheme with a view to improving the nation's health. Calcium, iron, minerals and vitamins had to be added to certain foods. The Emergency Milk and Meals scheme of 1941 supplemented basic rations with extra items for expectant mothers and young children. Cheap milk and cod liver oil and orange juice went to mothers; the price of milk and school meals was kept low by government subsidies; children unable to afford even subsidised foods, were given them free. The Prime Minister strongly approved of this policy, 'There is no finer investment for any community than putting milk into babies', he said.

Hospital care, so limited before the war, had to be extended to cope with the war-wounded who were given free treatment. The war-wounded could also include civilians injured by bombs. The local authority hospitals, and the hospitals set up by voluntary charities, soon had many 'emergency beds' whose occupants received treatment paid for by the state. A free immunisation programme soon produced a sizeable fall in deaths from diphtheria.

During the war prices rose quite sharply. The government tried to keep them down by paying subsidies to food producers, but old age pensioners found it especially hard to manage. In 1940 the unemployment Assistance Board was given power to pay supplementary amounts to needy elderly folk. This was the first step in widening the work of the Board and making it a more popular institution. The Board helped bombed families who could not support themselves in the disastrous circumstances following the destruction of their homes. In 1941, as a result of pressure from Ernest Bevin, the Board abolished the household means test. This detailed enquiry into the earnings of all the dependants of an unemployed man had always caused resentment; it disappeared at a time when the needs of war were sharply reducing unemployment.

Although these various welfare reforms were separate actions coping with separate problems, they pointed towards a much more general system of help to all people in need, organised and often paid for by the state. In 1942 a plan was published that carried this idea much further and offered, at last, an overall, organised view of the bits and pieces of welfare schemes that had grown up.

The Beveridge Report

The Second World War, like the First World War, encouraged people to discuss and hope for a reformed post-war Britain. Those eager to see a reconstructed country focussed their hopes, after December 1942, on the contents of a three hundred page book written by Sir William Beveridge. This Beveridge Report was the result of pressure from the TUC, which told the Labour minister, Arthur Greenwood, 'We are definitely of the opinion that the country cannot continue to afford the inefficient and incomplete services rendered to insured workers together with the expensive muddle and waste associated with it. We ask the Minister of Health to take the lead in an examination of the whole position with a view to plans being produced which would provide a properly balanced scheme.'

Beveridge's suggestions were the response to this pressure, for Greenwood gave him the task of leading a committee to study insurance and the resulting ideas were very much Beveridge's own notions. He wanted to see the whole system made much more simple and more efficient; he believed that insurance should protect people against all the serious hardships of life, and he thought that the scheme should cover the whole population of the country. The insurance payments he planned were seen as the rightful due of all, not money to be doled out carefully in differing amounts according to a means test. But he did not think payments should be generous. Beveridge was a Liberal, a believer in the insurance principle of people contributing to the savings organised by the state,

Signs of wartime welfare

1938	Nearly 3,000 deaths from diphtheria
1945	818 deaths from diphtheria
1940	130,000 school meals served daily
1945	1,650,000 school meals served daily

and if people wished to make a more generous provision for themselves then he believed they should turn to private insurance schemes.

He did not confine himself simply to looking at insurance. He argued that 'the organisation of social insurance should be treated as one part only of a comprehensive policy of social progress. Social insurance may provide income security, it is an attack on Want. But Want is one only of five giants. The others are Disease, Ignorance, Squalor, and Idleness.' To fight these giants Beveridge stated that it would be necessary to have a proper national health service, a policy of full employment, and allowances paid to families with children.

Beveridge said of his ideas, 'The scheme proposed here is in some ways a revolution but in more important ways it is a natural development from the past. It is a British Revolution.' He was criticised by the private insurance companies who felt his plans would hurt their business. One of their officials declared of the Report, 'The author is an economist turned spendthrift destroying every vestige of self reliance and self help.' The Prime Minister was worried about the cost of the proposals. The war was hurting Britain, yet, Churchill believed, post-war Britain needed strong defence forces to prevent another war. 'A dangerous optimism is growing up', he wrote, 'about the conditions it will be possible to establish after the war. Our foreign investments have almost disappeared. The United States will be a strong competitor. The question steals across the mind whether we are not committing our people to tasks beyond their capacity to bear.'

But there was no doubt about the general reaction to the Beveridge Report. Though it was written in dry and difficult

William Beveridge.
1879–1963. Educated at Charterhouse and Oxford, became an expert on unemployment problems and helped Churchill and Lloyd George with legislation on Labour Exchanges and insurance. Board of Trade official 1908, Director of Labour Exchanges 1909–16, Director of London School of Economics 1919–37. Served on several commissions and committees but especially led the investigation into insurance that produced the 'Report on Social Insurance and Allied Services'. This 'Beveridge Report' was a major talking point thereafter, helped shape Coalition policy and plans 1944–5 and Labour policy after 1945. Liberal M.P. 1944–5.

language, it became a best seller. The Labour Party and the trade unions welcomed it with enthusiasm. The Ministry of Information found it to be a major topic of conversation; its officials on Clydeside, for instance, reported, 'Interest in the Beveridge Plan on its publication was really tremendous. For a week or two the war news tended to take a back seat. Practically everyone approved of the underlying principles. Soldiers writing home spoke of their pleasure at the Scheme.'

In parliament, 97 Labour and 22 Conservative and Liberal MPs voted that the Report should be put into operation as soon as possible. One of them, the Labour MP James Griffiths, told the House, 'It is by acceptance or rejection of the plan that we shall be judged by the nation. I suggest that the question which we ought to ask ourselves is not whether we can afford the plan, but whether we can afford to face the post-war period without it.'

The end of the Coalition

The Coalition came to an end in the summer of 1945. By then it had made a start on one or two parts of the Beveridge

The Main Points of the Beveridge Report

1. The appointment of a minister to control all the insurance schemes.
2. A standard weekly payment by people in work as a contribution to the insurance fund.
3. The right to payments for an indefinite period for people out of work.
4. Old age pensions, maternity grants, funeral grants, pensions for widows and people injured at work.
5. Payments to be at a standard rate, the same for all whatever their private means, paid without a means test.
6. Family allowances to be introduced.
7. A national health service to be set up.

Report. In 1943 a ministry to supervise insurance had been set up, and in 1945 family allowances were agreed. These allowances were less generous than Beveridge had proposed, being 5s a week for every child after the first one, not 8s for every child without exception. The payment of these sums did not begin for another year.

By 1945 the Coalition had also created a Ministry of Town and Country Planning (1943). One of its first reports suggested the setting up of new towns to reduce congestion in London. Temporary homes were built, at state expense, for some of Britain's homeless, the price of building materials was controlled to stop house prices getting out of hand. In 1944 a Conservative, R. A. Butler, piloted through parliament a new Education Act. The act provided for free secondary education for all from the age of eleven (twelve in Scotland) up to the age of fifteen.

Not only were there these achievements, there were also Government White Papers showing what was planned in the near future. There were statements to show that a high and stable level of employment, and the creation of a national health service, were matters to which the government was committed. If the Coalition could agree on so much, then both Labour and Conservative Parties felt that social welfare policies must be pursued after the war.

When the general election was held in July 1945, voters found the promises in Labour's programme 'Let us Face the Future' more convincing. Labour concentrated on home affairs, stating it would reform industry, introduce the

HELP HIM FINISH THE JOB

We've beaten the Hun, But there's more to be done.

- We must defeat Japan.
- We must put Britain back on her feet again.
- We must co-operate with other nations to ensure that a durable peace follows victory.

These are tasks calling for sane and experienced statesmanship.

VOTE CONSERVATIVE

SUPPORT MR. CHURCHILL AND NATIONAL GOVERNMENT

3785   Printed and published by VACHER & SONS LTD., Westminster, S.W.1

The Conservative election campaign of 1945 leaned heavily on the popularity of Winston Churchill. Churchill believed that a Britain strong in world affairs was very important indeed.

LET'S BUILD THE HOUSES—QUICK !

Vote LABOUR X

left: *A Labour poster for the 1945 election showing a promise to build much-needed houses.*

Beveridge Report, provide homes, and keep full employment. The Conservatives relied heavily on Winston Churchill's personality, but though he was enormously popular for his wartime achievements, as a peacetime leader he seemed to have less to offer. Conservative policy included many social reforms, but voters remembered the pre-war slump years and treated their proposals cautiously. The election gave Labour, at last, a clear working majority with 393 MPs facing 213 Conservatives. The task ahead was enormous for the war had damaged the economy, destroyed property, and wrecked world trade, yet people hoped for a better life in the future. The veteran social reformer Seebohm Rowntree summed up the situation, saying: 'The whole of the social and economic life of the nation has been unrooted by the war as by an earthquake. When peace comes the social and economic evils and injustices for which the community suffered before the war must not be permitted in the new world which has to be created.'

THE LAND OF PROMISE

Lord Woolton (Conservative) and Ernest Bevin (Labour) are shown bearing promises based on Beveridge's plans. Both parties are making the most of the enthusiasm for Beveridge's reforms. A Punch cartoon of October 1944.

Summary of Key Steps

1940 Supplementary payments scheme for paying extra to old people.
1941 Emergency Milk and Meals Act. Extra food high in vitamins provided for mothers and young children.
1942 Beveridge Report. A plan to equip the country with a complete scheme to care for times of illness, old age and unemployment.
1943 Establishment of the Ministry of Town and Country Planning
1944 Education Act. Free secondary education was to be provided for all from 11 to 15 years (12 to 15 in Scotland).
1945 Family allowances scheme agreed. Extra money would be paid to families with 2 or more children.

7 The welfare state

Problems for the new government

Between 1945 and 1948 much of the modern welfare state was completed. Yet these were most difficult times for Britain; finding resources for welfare was far from easy. The Second World War had brought death and destruction directly to Britain itself. Not only were countless homes, schools and factories wrecked; essential services (such as the railways) and industries (especially coal) were exhausted and run-down.

The war had cost Britain much of her wealth: £1,000 million of foreign investments had been sold; exports had been halved, and Britain's merchant shipping had shrunk by a quarter. Yet Britain owed the USA over £3,000 million and desperately needed goods from the Americans with which to re-build, goods for which Britain was quite unable to pay. The USA had helped Britain during the war by 'Lend-Lease', allowing American goods to come to Britain with payment for them put off to some future and uncertain time. As soon as the war ended, so did Lend-Lease. It was hard to see how a country so deeply in debt, with exports that paid for less than one-fifth of her imports, could plunge into an expensive programme.

There was another strong call on Britain's resources. The post-war world seemed a most dangerous place; it was far too risky to disarm as rapidly as the country had done after 1918. Britain also paid money to Germany to relieve famine conditions. Even the weather was hostile! The winter of 1946–7 was quite exceptionally severe, and there was not enough coal to keep factories working and homes heated.

Tackling the problems

Clement Attlee's government was determined not to betray its election promises. Yet its programme of social reforms, industrial overhaul and a strong foreign policy was going to be very costly. Money had to be raised by keeping in peacetime the wartime controls on supplies. By nationalising coal, electricity, gas, the airways, the Bank of England, the railways and the waterways, the government kept a firm grip on a large part of the economy. Rationing not only continued, it became more severe; in 1947 for instance, potato rationing was introduced for the first time. The British people still had their food, fuel, and clothing tightly managed for them. The choice of goods in shops remained very limited; instead the government supported industry and urged industrialists to win as many export orders as they could.

Help also came from abroad, the economist J. M. Keynes was sent to seek an American loan. Although the loan was less than Britain had hoped to borrow, and included interest charges that Keynes had hoped to avoid, it was invaluable in helping Britain to pay for all that she needed to recover from the war. Unfortunately the Americans provided the loan on conditions that brought Britain trouble in 1947. In that year Britain had to allow her sterling currency to be freely changed into dollars by any investors in Britain who wished to take advantage of the ending of tight controls over British money. Since post-war America had prospered whilst Britain struggled, many investors rushed to change their money. The government had to step in and impose controls once again.

Between 1948 and 1951 further American aid flowed to Britain. By 1948 American leaders had become worried about the spread of Communism across the globe. By helping non-Communist countries grow in strength and prosperity they tried to build a barrier to Communism. Money flowed to

Help from abroad, 1945
The cancelling of the debt Britain had built up with the USA under the Lend-Lease scheme
An American loan of $3,750 millions at 2%
A Canadian loan of $1,500 millions

several lands, generally as a gift, Britain received about £2,400 million.

Throughout the 1945–51 period the country was free of serious unemployment problems save those temporarily caused by the quite exceptionally severe winter of 1946–7. However, the government's determination to keep Britain militarily strong did mean that social welfare reforms were not the only call upon the country's limited resources. Britain supported a large army, air force and navy; she kept bases across the world; atomic bombs were developed. There were also conflicts into which Britain was drawn. In Malaya British troops fought Communists and in Korea (in 1950) Britain joined in the effort made by several nations to defeat the invasion of South Korea by Communist North Korea. The expansion of welfare services should be seen against this background of problems and expenses. To push vigorously ahead in such times required both courage and optimism; at least British people seemed much more ready than after 1918 to wait for reforms to come and to accept the continuation of wartime controls into peace.

Insurance

James Griffiths was in charge of making Beveridge's plans for a simple comprehensive scheme of insurance a reality. Like Attlee, Griffiths saw his work as the completion of a process that had been going on for many years. A speech by the Conservative R. A. Butler showed that there were no big differences between Labour and Conservatives on this issue for Butler welcomed the scheme declaring, 'I think we should take pride that the British race has been able, shortly after the terrible period through which we have all passed together, to show the whole world that we are able to produce a social insurance scheme of this character.'

As Beveridge had suggested, the scheme involved weekly contributions from employees, employers and the state, and it paid benefits at standard rates. The cost of old age pensions had especially worried Beveridge. He had suggested there might be a twenty-year delay in bringing in pensions for men at 65 and women at 60 years; but Griffiths did not delay. He brought in the measure at once. As Beveridge had suggested, a scheme was introduced to provide compensation for people who were injured at work. The Industrial Injuries Act pro-

The main points of the 1946 National Insurance Act

Benefits   unemployment benefit, sickness benefit, maternity benefit, widow's benefit, guardian's allowance, retirement pension, death grant.

Rates of benefit   basic rate 26s a week, for a married man 42s, 7s 6d extra for the first child.

vided payments to those temporarily hurt and long-term payments for those put permanently out of a job. For the latter group, because an injured person might be put to extra expense, the rates of payment were more generous than for the unemployed. An injured man got 45s a week, with 16s for a wife and 7s 6d for each child.

In 1948 a National Assistance Board was set up to help people for whom the insurance scheme did not provide enough help, or the right kind of help. For some people the insurance benefits were simply not enough and as time passed this problem became increasingly serious. The insurance benefits did not rise sufficiently often to keep up with the now steadily rising cost of living and old people especially had to turn to the Assistance Board for further help. This help was given only to the needy; the Board's officials had to question the applicant to make sure that they were dealing with a genuine claim. This 'needs test' was less harsh than the old means test for it did not include a check on the earnings of other members of the claimant's family. The Board's help might consist of weekly payments, but it could also give single payments to solve a particular problem (such as an urgent need for bedding or clothing).

The insurance and national assistance schemes were huge undertakings. Thousands of new staff were needed, new offices had to be built, and the files and records of information about Britain's citizens began to grow.

The National Health Service

The new Minister of Health was Aneurin Bevan. By 1945 Bevan had won himself a considerable reputation as a very forthright speaker who held strong Socialist views. During the war he had been Churchill's most determined and persistent critic in parliament and Conservative politicians regarded him as a person of extreme views. His task of building a national health service meant that he had to win the co-operation of

Aneurin Bevan. 1897–1960. One of the thirteen children of a Welsh miner. Worked in the pits at 13. Active trade unionist, helped in the 1926 General Strike. From 1929 M.P. for Ebbw Vale as a left wing Labour M.P. Brilliant orator and frequent critic of Churchill's wartime government. 1945–51 Minister of Health responsible for introducing the National Health Service and tackling the post-war housing problem. Resigned when charges on some Health Service items were brought in and quarrelled quite often with the Labour leadership from 1950.

doctors. A great many of them, already worried about what a health service might do to their jobs, were even more concerned when faced by Aneurin Bevan. What doctors feared was that they would be turned into state officials, would lose independence, and would be sent to work wherever the government chose to place them.

Bevan brought in a bill in 1946 to outline the features of the health service he wished to set up, and allowed a two year delay before the service would start work. During this time he hoped to win over the majority of doctors. In introducing his bill Bevan pointed out that the old health insurance system

> 'covered only twenty-one million, the rest of the population have to pay whenever they desire the services of a doctor; the National Health Insurance scheme does not provide for the self-employed nor the families of dependants. It gives no backing to the doctor in the form of special services. Our hospital organisation has grown up with no plan. This Bill provides a universal health service with no insurance qualifications of any sort. It is intended that there shall be no limitations on the kind of assistance given – general practitioners' service, specialists, hospitals, eye treatment, dental treatment, hearing facilities.'

The detailed arrangements for the health service were then worked out in two years of discussion. When they actually met the man they had thought of as a fierce Welsh Socialist, doctors found him charming, witty, and ready to negotiate. Hospital staff were won over quite readily. Their buildings and medical equipment were so expensive and so much in need of overhaul and additions that they realised only the government could provide what they needed. Bevan agreed that hospital doctors could continue to treat private patients as well as working for the health service, and that hospitals should have a number of beds for patients who wanted to be treated privately and could afford to pay. The hospitals were organised in groups, each group controlled by a Regional Board appointed by the minister. Each hospital had a management committee to watch over its affairs. Major hospitals which were centres for the training of new doctors had their own separate governors whom the minister himself appointed.

Winning over GPs was not so easy. In 1946 a poll amongst them showed that 64% were opposed to Bevan's plans. The British Medical Association organised and led a campaign that argued that what was proposed would destroy doctors' freedom to treat patients as they thought right. But the doctors became increasingly isolated, for popular opinion ran very strongly in favour of the health service. Lord Moran, President of the Royal College of Physicians, helped Bevan gradually to calm doctors' fears. At times the discussion between the two sides became quite angry. (Bevan once called the BMA 'a small body of politically poisoned people'.) But by 1948 the detailed arrangements the minister was ready to make had persuaded a quarter of doctors in England and a third in Wales and Scotland to sign on for the new service. Early in 1948 organised opposition collapsed and the health service was able to come into operation on 5 July 1948.

The service that emerged was paid for, very largely, by taxes. The weekly insurance stamp did include a little for health insurance, but enough to pay only 9% of its cost in 1949, 10% by 1954. Bevan calmed doctors' worries about becoming state officials by agreeing not to pay them by direct salary. New doctors received some direct salary from the government, but in general the pay doctors received depended on the number of patients on their lists. When medical practices had been private, doctors had bought and sold them. Bevan insisted that this must stop, arguing that patients were

"Just spots before the eyes. . . . Don't worry, we'll soon cure that!"

left: *Not everyone welcomed the reforms to the nation's health service. The British Medical Association campaigned against the state control of medicine. A cartoon from the 'Daily Mirror'.*

below left: *Children being weighed at Woodberry Down Health Centre, October 1952. Bigger and healthier children were one of the results of the growth of social welfare.*

below right: *Britain's population had suffered for many years from tuberculosis, a disease that often affected the lungs of undernourished people living in overcrowded conditions. The improvement of living standards, together with X-ray checks on people's chests carried out by units like this helped to bring the disease under control by the 1950s.*

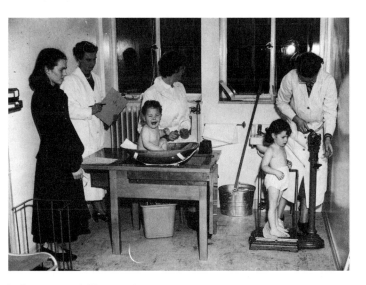

being treated like cattle. But he did set aside £66 million for doctors to draw upon when they retired, to compensate them for no longer being able to sell practices they had spent lifetimes building up. The work of GPs was henceforth watched over by Executive Councils set up in each county and borough and made up of equal numbers of medical and lay people.

Some aspects of health care were kept by local authorities.

Their Medical Officers supervised services such as vaccination, immunisation, health visiting, child care, and provision for the destitute (especially the elderly).

When the health service started it brought such a flood of people seeking treatment that Bevan himself declared, 'I shudder to think of the ceaseless cascade of medicines which is pouring down British throats at the present time.' Prescriptions had cost about £7 million a month before the health service was created; within three months they cost twice that figure and they continued to rise. Dentists had expected about four million patients a year yet twice that number sought treatment. The National Health Service became an increasingly heavy burden on British finances and, much as Bevan and some of his colleagues resented it, charges for some of its services had to be introduced by 1951.

Housing

Post-war Britain faced a huge housing shortage. The war damaged and destroyed thousands of homes and prevented normal house-building work from going ahead. Moreover the slum-clearing programme of the 1930s had barely begun to dent the problem of sub-standard housing. The burden of tackling the problem fell upon Bevan's Ministry of Health, yet the ministry had already more than enough to do in attempting to set up the National Health Service.

The ministry's first task was to house the homeless, and to this end it continued the Coalition policy of putting up temporary factory-made 'prefabricated' homes. This provided 157,000 dwellings, far too few to satisfy the country's needs. The fact that building supplies and skilled labour were not plentiful compelled Bevan to choose where to concentrate conventional house-building. He put the emphasis on the building of council houses for rent, placing severe restrictions on private building. People in homes that needed considerable spending to raise them to a decent level received help from the Treasury, but the fact remained that by 1951 there was still a very serious housing shortage in Britain.

The government's housing policy did show concern for the future, as well as efforts to meet an immediate need. Bevan insisted that the council houses must satisfy quite a high standard. In 1946 a New Towns Act set out plans for dealing with

Harlow New Town was one of the first eight towns planned after the 1946 New Towns Act. The photograph shows three-storey flats (left) and three-bedroomed terraced houses. The Harlow Art Trust commissioned the sculpture from Barbara Hepworth.

overcrowding in older cities. New communities were to be carefully designed and built, with government help; initially twelve were planned by 1950. In 1947 the Town and Country Planning Act gave counties and county boroughs much more power to plan their communities, and to buy up properties in areas that they wanted to re-develop. The government's life ended before really massive signs were visible of what it proposed, but in the following years the re-building of old communities and the creation of new ones went ahead on the basis of these post-war plans.

Child welfare

By 1947 the Education Act of 1944 was in operation. The government raised the leaving age to fifteen at a time when the country was short of workers, it also had to spend more of its precious resources on school-building and on an emergency programme to train enough teachers to staff the schools. Schools were organised so that at eleven (twelve in Scotland) children were examined and divided between grammar schools for the most able, and secondary modern schools for the majority. The Education Act proposed a third kind of school – a technical school – but not many of these were provided. The idea of sorting children into different schools on the basis of an examination did arouse a little criticism at the time. By 1947 the London County Council in particular had become unhappy about the system and planned comprehensive schools instead. London's first comprehensive, Kidbrooke School, opened in 1954. The government also planned a big increase in opportunities in higher education. Universities and colleges were to be expanded and there was to be a system of grants from the state or the local authority so that students able to win higher education places could accept them even if their parents had little money.

In 1948 the Children Act tried to provide a better service for children who needed special care and protection. Local authorities were now required to appoint Children's Officers whose job it would be to see that children taken into the local authorities' care were decently housed, and properly cared for.

The range of reforms carried through by 1950 adds up to a system that is generally called 'the Welfare State'. The closing stages of this work were supervised by Labour Party ministers, but they knew very well that what they were doing was building on foundations laid by Liberals and Conservatives. The care of people in need and the improvement of people's health, housing and education were policies that statesmen of all three parties had at times thought necessary. When a Conservative government replaced Labour in 1951 it did not at once start attacking the social reforms of the previous five years but accepted these reforms and even added further improvements.

Certainly the health, housing and education of the British people have been much improved during the twentieth century. In 1950 Seebohm Rowntree carried out a third study of York and found far less overcrowding and poverty. Whereas poor pay and unemployment had once been the main cause of poverty, by 1950 it was the elderly who formed the main group of the poor. Even for them life was far more comfortable than it had been fifty years earlier. A great deal of money had been spent and large numbers of officials had been appointed to make the system work. Far more people paid taxes; taxes were fixed at higher rates; controls over people's lives were more detailed and numerous and the power of the government was increased. But everyday life, for the majority of people, was vastly improved.

Summary of Key Steps

1946 National Insurance Act

1946 National Health Act. In 2 years' time a free and comprehensive health service was to be set up.

1947 Town and Country Planning Act. More power given local authorities to plan their housing properly.

1948 National Assistance Act. Setting up of a Board to provide extra aid for those not adequately helped by insurance.

1948 Children Act. A better system of caring for children in need was introduced.

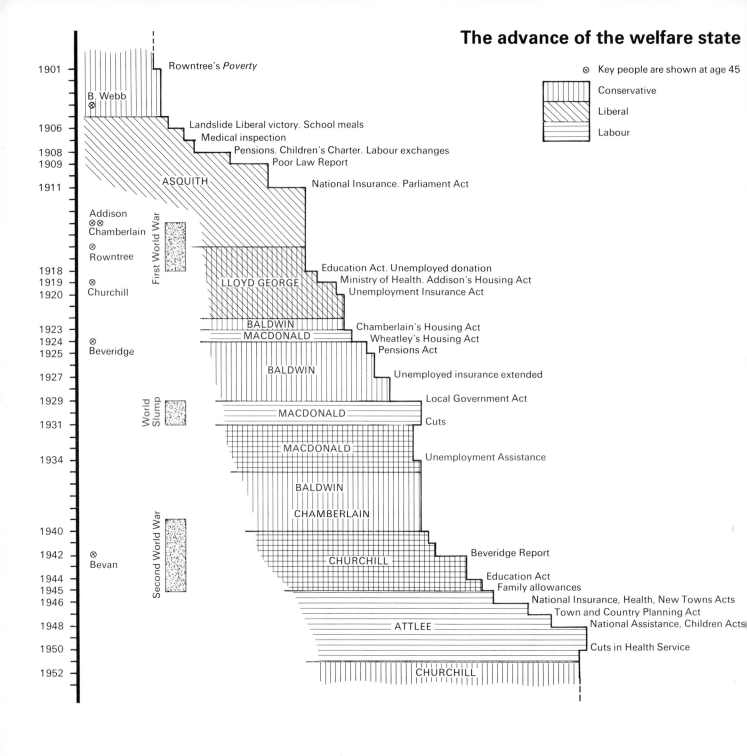

The advance of the welfare state

⊗ Key people are shown at age 45

Conservative

Liberal

Labour

1901 — Rowntree's *Poverty*

B. Webb
⊗

1906 — Landslide Liberal victory. School meals

Medical inspection

1908 — Pensions. Children's Charter. Labour exchanges
1909 — Poor Law Report

1911 — National Insurance. Parliament Act

ASQUITH

Addison
⊗⊗
Chamberlain

⊗
Rowntree

First World War

1918 — Education Act. Unemployed donation
1919 — Ministry of Health. Addison's Housing Act
⊗ Churchill
1920 — Unemployment Insurance Act

LLOYD GEORGE

1923 — BALDWIN — Chamberlain's Housing Act
1924 — MACDONALD — Wheatley's Housing Act
⊗ Beveridge
1925 — Pensions Act

1927 — BALDWIN — Unemployed insurance extended

1929 — Local Government Act

World Slump

MACDONALD

1931 — Cuts

1934 — MACDONALD — Unemployment Assistance

BALDWIN

CHAMBERLAIN

1940 —

Second World War

1942 — Beveridge Report
⊗
Bevan
CHURCHILL

1944 — Education Act
1945 — Family allowances
1946 — National Insurance, Health, New Towns Acts
Town and Country Planning Act
1948 — ATTLEE — National Assistance, Children Acts

1950 — Cuts in Health Service

1952 — CHURCHILL